d25

SLS

Human Resources, Employment and Development Volume 1: The Issues

The Fifth Congress of the International Economic Association had concerned itself with the world's physical resources and their implications for growth and development. It was natural that the Sixth Congress should go on to examine the problems of human development, regarding the human participants not primarily as factors in development and production, but more importantly as the ultimate beneficiaries from development.

This first of the five volumes in which the work of the Congress is being published contains a review of the work of the Congress as a whole by Professor Shigeto Tsuru and four broad-ranging addresses to the plenary sessions of the Congress. In the first of these, Professor Józef Pajestka, drawing on the thinking and experience of Poland, describes the ways in which, in a planned economy, the strategy should be made to ensure that man as a beneficiary is considered at every stage. Pierre Maillet of France and Armando Labra of Mexico comment on his arguments.

In the second of these plenary addresses, Raul Prebisch summarises and develops his ideas regarding the dominating influences of the self-interested technologies and economic institutions of the powerful countries of the centre over the weak, imitative and self-accommodating countries of the periphery. Prebisch's ideas and ways of thinking predominated, perhaps inevitably, throughout a congress held in a Latin-American country. Jagdish Bhagwati and Bo Södersten were the two invited to comment and both of them in different ways challenge Prebisch's identification of particular political regimes with particular types of economic system. But this immensely important issue runs through much of the subsequent work of the congress.

Paul Samuelson's fascinating address discusses 'The World Economy at Century's End'. He takes Keynes and Schumpeter as his major prophets, contrasts them and their views of world trends. He himself would like to see the predominance of the economically rational mixed economy. But both he and his two commentators, Herbert Giersch and Tigran Khachaturov, find themselves driven back to Prebisch's questions: do particular types of economy presuppose particular types of political regime?

In the fourth plenary address, Professor Tsuru himself provides a most interesting account of the changes in social and human relations that accompanied and made possible the Meiji Restoration and the rapid economic development of Japan that followed. He shows how the various manpower and managerial requirements were met and how a continuity of change from status to contract made possible a type of capitalism remarkably different from that of western countries. Professors Onitiri and Contini draw lessons for the developing world.

This first volume is completed by four addresses to the final sessions of the Congress. Two of these, by Dr Flores de la Peña and Lord Kaldor, return to the same problems of the long-term trends of the world economy as had been discussed by Paul Samuelson and his commentators. Dr de la Peña, as might be expected, is primarily concerned with the great Latin-American issue of the relation of regimes to systems and institutions and the dependence of liberal economies on political dictatorships. Kaldor finds more grounds for pessimism than optimism in a world threatened by nuclear war and constrained by limits of natural resources.

This volume forms an introduction to the four volumes which publish the principal papers presented and discussed in the six sections into which the Congress divided.

Professor Shigeto Tsuru, the editor of this volume, learned his economics at Harvard under Schumpeter. He was, first, Professor of Economics and later President of Hitotsubashi University. Author of many books and articles, chiefly in the field of the economic development of Japan, he was President of the International Economic Association, 1977–80, and architect of the Congress recorded in this and its associated volumes.

Human Resources, Employment and Development
Volume 1: The Issues

Proceedings of the Sixth World Congress
of the International Economic Association
held in Mexico City, 1980

Edited by
SHIGETO TSURU
President, 1977–80

First published 1983 by
THE MACMILLAN PRESS LTD
London and Basingstoke
Companies and representatives
throughout the world

ISBN 0 333 32735 7

Printed in Hong Kong

Contents

ADDRESSES TO THE CLOSING SESSIONS

Acknowledgements

The Congress that is recorded in this and four other volumes was made possible by the generosity of the Mexican authorities, who, under the auspices of His Excellency the President of Mexico, José López Portillo, contributed almost the totality of the costs of the Congress including contributions to the cost of transporting and accommodation of two hundred of the invited participants. We are especially grateful to Manuel Aguilera Gómez, President of the Colegio Nacional de Economistas of Mexico, who with the local Organising Committee took care of all local arrangements. Without their enthusiastic help we could never have dealt with the immense problems of handling the arrangements for the very large numbers of participants and for making available the papers of the conference.

As always we must express our gratitude to UNESCO and the Ford Foundation whose general grants to the IEA were used to defray some of the expenses incurred by the IEA secretariat.

Finally our thanks are due to the International Programme Committee which, under the guidance of our President Shigeto Tsuru, was responsible for drawing up the scientific programme and selecting the paper writers and the group organisers. Our thanks are also due to the many authors of papers presented to the different sections of the Congress.

Introduction

Shigeto Tsuru

The Sixth World Congress of economists organised by the International Economic Association was held in Mexico City on 4 to 8 August 1980 with the general subject of 'Human Resources, Employment and Development'. This volume contains the record of the scientific presentations in the opening plenary session, consisting of the four invited papers and the two comments on each one of them; it contains in addition several addresses to the closing plenary session. As the retiring President of the Association, I also spoke in that closing session; but I did so more or less extemporaneously, mainly to express our gratitude to the Local Organising Committee in Mexico for the preparation and the manifold support it had provided, thus making our Congress a real success. I simply repeat these words here, having decided, in my capacity as editor of this volume, not to reconstruct in writing what I said on that occasion.

The general theme for the Sixth Congress was decided at the time of the Fifth Congress in 1977 in Tokyo where the general subject of 'Economic Growth and Resources' was chosen, deliberately setting aside the problem of *human resources* for future discussion. Thus the Association owed it to its member associations to carry out this predetermined task in the next Congress to follow that in Tokyo. To give effect to this, an international scientific programme committee was organised with the following membership:

Shigeto Tsuru (Japan), Chairman
Rodolfo Becerril Straffon (Mexico), Co-Chairman
Samir Amin (Senegal)
Mary Jean Bowman (USA)
Michel Debeauvais (France)

Harold Gerfin (Federal Republic of Germany)
Tigran Khachaturov (USSR)
Gunther Kohlmey (Democratic Republic of Germany)
Gautam Mathur (India)

Franco Modigliani (USA)   Paul Streeten (UK, World Bank)
H. M. A. Onitiri (Nigeria)   Lorie Tarshis (Canada)
Harry Oshima (USA,   Victor E. Tokman (Argentina)
   Philippines)   Victor L. Urquidi (Mexico)
Mark Perlman (USA)

For the opening plenary sessions, four major speakers were chosen with an eye to achieving balanced geographical representation: one each from Eastern Europe, the western advanced market economies, Latin America and Asia. And again a balance was sought in the choice of discussants for each of the four major papers, as readers can confirm in the later pages of this volume.

The specialised sessions, which followed the opening plenary session, were divided into the six following groups, which worked simultaneously:

    I. Human Resources: Concepts and Measurement
   II. Human Resources and Employment in Developing Countries
 III. Human Resources and Employment in Developed Countries
 IV. International Economy and Employment
   V. Human Resources in the Long-term Perspective
 VI. Employment and Development in Latin America

On past occasions we have included in the first volume of the congress proceedings the summary reports by the chairmen of these specialised groups presented in the final session of the congress. This time we have decided that these summary reports should take the form of introductions by the chairmen concerned to the four other proceedings volumes of the Mexico Congress, two of which will cover the work of two of the above groups in one volume: that is, I and V, III and IV; II and VI are each covered by separate volumes. Professor Urquidi's address in the closing plenary session, included here, in fact contains a succinct summary appraisal of these various specialised sessions.

It was perhaps inevitable that the four main speakers in the opening plenary session, though forewarned of the general theme of the Congress, should choose to range rather widely over the economic issues of current interest, not exclusively focused upon the problems of human resources and employment. There were, however, two issues to which more than one speaker paid close attention. One was the evaluation of the human factor in the process of economic development; the other was the relevance of institutional arrangements to the dynamics of development.

Pajestka, in particular, starts with the basic proposition that 'economic development is tantamount to the development of people – of their skills, capabilities, of their resourcefulness and motivations'. He is quite candid in admitting that socialism weakened some of the traditional human motivations, by eliminating unemployment and developing a broad and extensive system of social security. Furthermore, socialism has rejected the motivations of a competitive market system and of individual self-interest. He writes that 'all those motivations have to be substituted by other motivations, if the overall societal drive for progress is not to be diminished'.

What, then, are the substitutive motivations? Pajestka does not answer this question directly. Instead, he draws our attention to another aspect of the evaluation of the human factor in the process of economic development: the 'ends' to be sought as the result of the development process rather than as the 'means' to the achievement of that process. Thus enters the concept of 'human needs', which is interpreted quite broadly to include, besides economic goods and services, 'needs of expression, of creativity, of participation, of justice, of harmony and beauty, and the like'. When these needs are recognised as essential, that recognition can be a bridge to the motivation for efforts and exertion on the part of individuals as well as of the society as a whole.

Commenting on this line of thinking, Labra, while applauding the broadening of the concept of 'human needs', expressed his regret at the absence in Pajestka's presentation of 'a conceptual bridge between needs and concrete forms of a social motivational scheme'. That 'bridge', according to Labra, has to be 'eminently political', and our task is 'to propose forms of political organisation that can rally popular support and demands'. In particular, Labra stresses, as 'the most important vehicle of change for the new strategy', the effective use of 'the pressure that the independent and organised working class can impose upon public power decisions'.

Maillet's comments on Pajestka, on the other hand, are somewhat more cautious. For example, on the problem of 'What People Can Do', he appears to be painfully aware of various constraints (a monoculture economy, energy, and the like) that each nation is confronted with and is particularly concerned with the fact that 'the great bulk of today's research in the world, and with it the direction of tomorrow's technological progress for a quarter of a century to come, is shaped to fit the scale of values of one single country', by implication that of the

United States of America. As regards the motivation scheme and economic system also, Maillet proposes to abandon 'the idea of a single development model' and instead 'to place the most vigorous stress on the variety of possible types of development, and on the advantage of preserving that variety in the interests of mankind as a whole'.

Another paper which focused on the evaluation of the human factor in the process of economic development was that by Tsuru. Not because it was my own, but because it is more of a historical narrative, any summary of the paper itself may be omitted here. But the highlights of the comments by the two discussants are worth recording.

For Contini, Tsuru's paper brought out three crucial aspects of the role of human resources in the history of Japanese development: first, the role of education; second, the role of women's participation in factory work in the early stages of the industrialisation process; and third, the role of the political system. This third point is specified further to mean that 'in the early stages of Japan's industrialisation the political system did have a clear-cut strategy laid down: breaking the privileges of feudal classes and at the same time *making use of the traditional values* to lead the way towards rapid development' (my italics). Contini considers the italicised element as crucially important. Further, he makes the empirical observation that in all the less developed countries in the last twenty years or so there has been a definitely positive correlation between a high participation rate of women and the achievement of rapid growth of GNP and exports. One wonders if this is because of the possibility of exploiting women's cheap labour, as was the case in Japan. Another empirical finding Contini reports is extremely interesting: that is, the relative amount of employment in the tertiary sectors as well as the relative income earned in them, as compared with the manufacturing sector, are, on the whole, *higher* in less developed countries. He attempts to explain this by pointing out that 'in many of the countries which have yet to reach a consolidated industrial structure, the role of ensuring social equilibrium and political consensus is very often entrusted to the national bourgeoisie which operate mainly in the private tertiary sectors and in the public sector'. Statistically, Contini's finding can be corroborated by Japan's early industrialisation period also; but his explanation may have to be scrutinised further.

Onitiri's comments on Tsuru were laid out from the standpoint of attempting to draw lessons from the Japanese experience for the present-day developing countries. With necessary caution dictated by the difference in time and circumstances, he points to the following 'lessons' that can be learned with profit: first, the importance of keeping constant watch over the benefits obtained from the exploitation and exporting of raw materials; second, the advantage of 'a close working relationship between government and private enterprise', and third, the importance of 'moderating the growth of money incomes while maintaining a high level of productivity'. Onitiri was probably prompted to make these points chiefly by his concern over the problems faced with many of the developing countries today. He comes back, however, to the main thrust of Tsuru's paper and ends his comments by stressing the overriding importance of 'the rapid development of human resources' (including education) with a ringing phrase: 'The most valuable resource any country has is its people, the means and the end of economic advance'.

Two other major papers, those of Prebisch and Samuelson, had a much broader scope than the general theme of our congress. Thus, the editor of this volume may be excused for being somewhat selective in the coverage of the issues on which they expatiated. There was one issue which kept on reappearing, not only in these two papers, but also through the entire course of our congress discussions; that was the relevance of institutional arrangements to the dynamics of development. And Prebisch's paper provided a most systematic, though succinct, analysis of this problem in terms of the global dynamics of 'the centres' and 'the periphery'.

Prebisch's thesis is that capitalism has proved to be essentially 'centripetal' in the sense that 'the centres' not only have exploited 'the periphery' but also have imposed their patterns of consumption and life-styles, institutions and ideology on 'the periphery'. Thus capitalism in the 'periphery' has proved to be essentially imitative. The surplus produced there was either syphoned off to 'the centres' or appropriated by the indigenous upper-income brackets which tended to imitate the consumption pattern of 'the centres' with the consequence of frittering away the opportunities for accumulation. With the rise of the middle classes and the formation of trade unions, the distributive battle became acute in 'the periphery' and the 'conflictive' nature of the system became increasingly pronounced in the interplay of power relations. A political solvent for this situation was 'an inflationary spiral of a social nature'. The only way out is the transformation of the system itself. There are two options here. One is that the state takes over the ownership and management of the means of production, and the other is that 'the state uses the surplus with collective rationality'. Prebisch prefers the latter, calling this 'a synthesis of socialism and liberalism'—'socialism in the sense that the state regulates accumulation and distribution' and 'liberalism in that it basically postulates economic freedom closely bound up with political liberty in its original philosophic sense'.

Although Prebisch does not say so explicitly, Bhagwati, commenting on his paper, brought out a most compelling issue in Latin America today: 'Is there an inherent connection between the growth of authoritarian regimes and the spread of global capitalism to the periphery?' Or 'is it possible for economic liberalism to flourish if the political regime is not authoritarian?' This same point was referred to by Samuelson as 'maximal market freedoms under dictatorships' and also by Aguilera in his closing plenary speech when he said that in some of the developing economies they are trying 'through the iron fist of military regimes to turn the clock back and apply a sort of Manchester economic liberalism'. Bhagwati does concede that capitalism in 'the periphery' when combined with political pluralism, is subject to serious pressures and since such macro-pressures are rather difficult to handle in a democratic set-up, there is likely to be a resort to force or a kind of macro-discipline as 'politics of scarcity'. However, Bhagwati doubts if there are any 'deterministic laws relating the iron fist to the invisible hand' and cites the example of India where 'the authoritarian phase was extremely short-lived and was characterised by a remarkable return to political democracy plus a firmer commitment to economic liberalism'. Still, Prebisch's vision of the socialisation of 'flows' rather than of 'stocks' remains as a challenging strategy of transformation for developing countries today, if not for all capitalist societies.

On this transformation strategy proposed by Prebisch, Södersten comments that it 'seems to be reminiscent of a system of workers' control or a system of a labour-managed economy'. But the present editor feels that Prebisch may not quite agree with this interpretation. Otherwise, Södersten's comments on Prebisch are highly relevant to the 'centre-periphery' thesis of the latter, in that his observations lead us to modify the thesis because 'the industrial countries are no longer undisputed leaders in the world economy'. The reason for this is that the oil-producing countries and the so-called NICs – the new industrialised countries – have come to the forefront as new centres of economic power over the last decade. New problems of dynamic adjustment have thus arisen in the world economy, entailing, in the new light, such age-old issues as import substitution, transfer and income redistribution, all of which happen to have been Prebisch's special concern in the past. One only regrets that the congress did not provide a sufficient occasion for discussions between the authors of major papers and those who commented on them.

Samuelson's paper, like that of Prebisch, is concerned, not specifically with the general theme of the congress – that of 'Human Resources and Employment' – but with the relevance of institutional arrangements in the dynamics of development. Samuelson's thesis is essentially a case for the viability and efficacy of the mixed economy. For example, he says that 'the miracle decades of the 1950s and 1960s were actually *enhanced* by those encroachments of the mixed economy on laissez faire capitalism' and that 'all around the world, the post-Keynesian environment provided macroeconomic stimulus to employment and gave effective protection against deflation and persisting slump'. Samuelson, however, is not simply championing the cause of the mixed economy; in fact, his analysis goes deeper and points out the inevitability, as it were, of the mixed economy by saying that 'the same self-interest that provided the gasoline to make the classical game of markets operate must be expected *in today's political sphere* to motivate interferences with the laissez faire scenario' (italics added). This same observation leads him to state that 'stagflation is an intrinsic characteristic of the mixed economy' for the reason that the mixed economy is 'now a humane society'. No doubt, stagflation is an undesirable feature; and there seems to be no easy solution, and the impatient mind might say: 'Get rid of democracy and impose upon society the market regime!' But Samuelson's 'dream is to make the mixed economy work better . . . . to retain and promote the humane qualities of the mixed economy while conserving the efficiencies of the market mechanism'.

The title of Samuelson's paper was 'The World Economy at Century's End'; but he did not quite fill the frame given by this title. Thus, Giersch, commenting on it, chose to give his own prognostications on the problems which the world economy is likely to face towards the end of this century. But first, he dealt with the problem of the mixed economy which was Samuelson's main concern. With characteristic continental doctrinal sophistication, as well as that drawn from his forty years experience in the German civil service, Giersch asks bluntly the question: 'What is so exciting about the mixed economy?' To him, the real issue of the mixed economy is – apart from stagflation – 'the unhappy choice between equity and efficiency' while economists are 'incapable of defining rules for the optimum division of labour between governments and markets which are sufficiently operational'. What is 'the optimum division' is the question which has not yet been answered in a systematic fashion. For one thing, Samuelson is so preoccupied, according to Giersch, with effective demand and with fiscal policy that he has left out of the picture the role of private autonomous investment and of the Schumpeterian entrepreneur.

On the stagflation problem, also, Giersch's explanation differs from that of Samuelson, in that he places major blame on politicians who 'have been made to believe in the existence of a stable non-vertical Phillips curve', and calls for a separate institution or instrument to deal with *each* of the two conflicting targets of low unemployment and price level stability.

As for the detailed analysis given by Giersch of the prospect of the world economy, filling the gap Samuelson left out, a mere summary may not do justice to the rich contents spelt out in his paper. But one point he stresses is worth calling to the attention of our readers: the point that 'the humane quality' of the mixed economy Samuelson speaks of is essentially for the benefit of compatriots, and perhaps even only for those who belong to the same pressure group, and that 'the real class conflict of our age is between labour in LDCs and labour in advanced countries'.

Khachaturov also, commenting on Samuelson's paper, divides his comment into two parts: the first part dealing with some of the issues raised by Samuelson, and the second part with the main theme of the congress, that of human resources. As regards the former, the prospect of the world economy in the coming two decades, he first makes the general observation that the 'miraculous mid-century sprint' had been made possible by the impact of rapid technological progress which was now slowing down; he then goes on specifically to focus on the prospect for the socialist world. He admits that 'there is also a slowing down in the economy of socialist countries' due to 'the expiration of the extensive factors of growth'. But he seems to be confident that 'socialist countries have large reserves of further growth, thanks to advantages of the planning system which provides the possibility of the full use of these reserves'. Khachaturov's prognosis for the annual rate of growth of Soviet industry until the end of the century is 4.2 per cent as a minimum.

On the human resources problem, Khachaturov considers in particular the question of the so-called population explosion. He regards the phenomenon of population growth in a positive light as 'the result of the improvement of people's health and well-being manifesting one of the achievements of the human civilisation'. He can do so because he is confident that unemployment can be eliminated under socialism and the food shortage can be overcome with proper management of land resources and the application of scientific knowledge. In fact, he is optimistic enough to say that 'the developing countries are nowadays in a far better position than was the socialist world at the beginning of its industrialisation period'. It would again have been interesting if we could have had a discussion between Prebisch and Khachaturov on this subject.

An innovation implemented at the closing plenary session of our Congress was the decision by the Local Organising Committee to have two distinguished economists present papers as guest speakers. They were H. Flores de la Peña of Mexico and Nicholas Kaldor of the United Kingdom. Both spoke on the subject of the world economic outlook, each with his characteristic analytical insight and profound knowledge of reality. To them, the International Economic Association is most grateful and the present editor is happy to be able to include the texts of those two papers in this volume.

In addition, readers will note that the texts of two other addresses are appended here. One is by Manuel Aguilera Gómez, Chairman of the Local Organising Committee, and the other is by Victor Urquidi, the new President of our Association. Both went far beyond mere ceremonial remarks to develop substantive, stimulating ideas which can fittingly be considered as an integral part of this volume.

One final word. Although my address in the closing session as retiring President of the Association is not included here, I may be permitted to mention one point on which I dwelt on that occasion. I said, among other things, something like the following: 'Listening to Professor Nicholas Kaldor this morning, I cannot but recall the days in the 1930s when we were together at Harvard University. Paul Samuelson was also there at the time. Those were the days when young economists in their twenties or early thirties were gathered together in one capacity or another at Harvard. Other than the two I have just mentioned, there were Fritz Machlup, Wassily Leontief, Oskar Lange, Georgescu-Roegen, Kenneth Boulding, Robert Triffin, Paul Baran – each from a different country. And I may also mention John D. Wilson whose son has made a brilliant contribution to one of the sessions in this Congress. As Samuelson wrote somewhere, these young economists did more to Harvard than Harvard did to them, which means that young economists in their twenties and thirties opened up and extended the frontier of economic science by challenging the then established mainstream economics and developing new analytical tools and paradigms. Today, the discipline of economic science may be in a similar stage to that of the 1930s, and a host of brilliant young economists are in a position to challenge the authority in our field. At least, I should like to hope so.'

I have not chosen to reconstruct this part of my address without a reason. It had been my suggestion, in pursuance of the above line of thinking, that we should organise a special session of critical appraisal by young economists of the entire deliberations of the congress to take place in the closing plenary. The suggestion was taken up by the executive committee of our Association; and we went on to canvass for possible economists from all over the world. Some dozen names were preliminarily selected, and the Association was ready officially to make contacts with them, believing that such an arrangement would set up a good precedent for bridging, even if partially, an inevitable generation gap in our ever-progressing discipline. Unfortunately, however, we were not able to carry out this innovation for a number of reasons for which no one is to be blamed. Oftener than not, it has been the case in the past that major innovational ideas in our discipline have been produced and developed by economists in the 'inimitable age of the twenties' as Schumpeter would say. I have a feeling that this tradition, which is as old as Isaac Newton in the field of natural science, continues to operate today. I can only say *Nunc Dimittis* as I retire from the Presidency of our Association.

Addresses to the Plenary Sessions

1 Basing Development Strategy on the Human Factor

Józef Pajestka

POLAND

I THE ESSENTIALS OF A DEVELOPMENT STRATEGY

We come to an international gathering such as this World Congress of economists most probably with the main aim of gaining some new inspirations in economic thinking. Openness to new concepts, new ways of understanding reality, new methods of analysis, are very much needed, particularly at the present juncture in the historical development process. We are facing, probably more than ever before, new facts and new challenges; and new horizons are appearing before humanity. To guide our behaviour, in response to all that, requires first and foremost appropriate patterns of understanding reality and its trends. And that is what we are, or should be, looking for.

The International Economic Association has directed our attention – for this congress – to the interrelationships between the human factor and the development process. This is a problem area of primary concern for evaluating the relevance of economic theorising and for formulating new approaches. It touches upon the very essence of the development process: its aims and its moving forces. It should therefore be seen as being at the very core of any development thinking, and any development strategy. This is, at least, how I understand the subject under discussion. The forthcoming observations are based on this understanding.

Any one of us taking part in international debates has a certain background: it comes from a certain school of economic thinking and is building on a certain type of socio-economic experience. My own

3

background is formed primarily by the actual development experience of the socialist countries of Eastern Europe and its underlying theoretical premises. This can certainly be seen throughout this paper, though its subject matter is not limited to the socialist development pattern alone. It is my belief that certain more general observations and propositions can be formulated, building on the socialist countries development approach and experience. In presenting them I retain the position of 'openness' formulated above.

The term 'development strategy' is of relatively recent origin in the vocabulary of economics; it is used today in reference not only to national development but also to international development.

Conceptual notions are always value-laden, and this is also true of the notion of the 'development strategy'. It implies the active shaping, or guiding, of the development process according to certain long-term goals for which appropriate ways and means are designed. Unless one accepts that, talking of a strategy would seem meaningless.

It can be seen that the term 'development strategy' came to be used in economic analysis as a result of the acceptance of the paradigm of conscious, purposeful shaping of the development process, or of development planning. This paradigm, which is of socialist origin, has been widely accepted nowadays, though its meaning is far from uniform.

While, however, the desirability of purposeful shaping of the development process is widely accepted, it is not always fully realised what this demands from economics and what schools of economic thinking are most suitable for it. Let us consider a few issues in this context.

Purposeful shaping of the development process requires the existence of a certain community of aims in a given system, a national economy, an international grouping, a world community. Factors making for that are of a societal, economic, institutional and political nature. They also determine various features of the functioning of any system subject to guidance, and the character of the guidance itself. Theories that ignore such factors can hardly be expected to contribute much to strategy design. Thus if, for instance, a theory assumes only two agents operating in the economic arena, firms and consumers, and concentrates on analysing their interplay, it is bound to be of little use for strategy design. The so-called institutional approach, on the other hand, can be more productive.

The character of the process of economic development seems a most appropriate conception for strategy design. It has to be assumed that the development process is not historically predetermined, but that it is capable of being influenced. This follows the concept of socio-economic change. Engineering this change, which implies among other things bringing new societal and economic forces into operation, becomes the main concern for strategy design. One may observe that if economics is concerned primarily with economic equilibrium and related problems, it does not have much to offer in this respect.

Forward looking is inevitable for any guidance of economic activity. The framing of strategy requires particularly long-term vision. Economic thinking is not always ready for that. Some economic schools shy away from long-term considerations. A short-term Keynesian approach to economic regulation should be particularly mentioned in this context. The long-term is of the very nature of strategic thinking. It can be much aided by long-term historical analysis, and requires the consideration of long-term prospectives.

Policy orientation is often lacking in economic discussion. This seems particularly true of the most refined theorising. Strategic thinking, on the other hand, necessitates the grasping of real policy issues, even if they are not readily amenable to elegant, theoretical treatment.

It is just in the context of the role of the human factor and of interhuman relations in the development process that a strategic view is very much required. Without that, and particularly without seeing the strategic role of the human factor in socio-economic change, development policy may lose its proper general orientation and fail to achieve socially meaningful and efficient progress in the long run.

It should be observed, on the other hand, that perception of the strategic role of the human factor in the development process is not a common characteristic of economic theorising. This seems particularly true of the quantitative analysis of economic development. In many, if not most, of the quantitative growth models, economic growth is presented as a function of capital-formation and import capability. Hence the so-called 'gaps theory' is developed, concerned with the two gaps – the savings gap and the balance of payments gap – as the critical obstacles to the development of the developing countries. True or not, and this cannot be judged in purely theoretical terms since quantitative theoretical constructs are always related to certain patterns of economic development, this theoretical approach does not hold out hopeful prospects for the developing countries. They can hope for 'transfers' bridging the gaps; but even if these were forthcoming, they could not possibly solve the development problems of the majority of the developing nations. It is in this light that a search for new development patterns has developed. It relies on different theoretical premises from those underlying the quantitative growth models.

The new thinking, appearing recently under the names of 'another development', 'alternative development patterns', 'self-reliance', 'internally generated development', and the like introduces the issue of strategic options with respect to the most fundamental development policies. The main option is seen in a shift from external to internal development factors and resources. This raises the problem of manpower utilisation, regarded from the aspect of quantitative development factors, and the wider problem of the role of the human factor and of interhuman relations in the development process, regarded from the broader vista of the socio-economic forces making for progress.

This idea of manpower utilisation for the sake of faster and better progress is not new in economic thinking. It has been widely seen that in most of the developing countries people are the great asset that is not fully used. To achieve full utilisation is, however, far from simple. It requires that the development process shall be guided by social interests, it requires adequate socio-economic change and political forces to carry it through, and it also requires certain important economic and managerial measures. It is probably because of these conditions that there have been hesitations to treat full manpower utilisation as a real strategic option. This does not mean that economic thinking has failed to give theoretical support to this proposition. Both broad concepts of manpower utilisation, and specific arguments, for instance regarding the choice of technology and labour-intensive technology, have been advanced. We are probably close to complete agreement regarding manpower utilisation as a practicable and desirable strategic objective; the new thinking I have described has contributed greatly to this.

A manpower utilisation strategy should not be seen, however, in narrow economic terms. Its proper dimension appears when set within the context of socio-philosophical considerations, seeing human beings both as the main source and as the main agent of progress. The basic proposition is that economic development is tantamount to the development of people – of their skills, capabilities, of their resourcefulness and motivations; without development of people there can be no economic development in the long run. Manpower utilisation is only one aspect of the role of the human factor in the development process.

There is in the socialist countries a vast body of experience connected with designing and implementing a development strategy concentrated on the human factor. Strangely enough, it is widely ignored. Let me present some lessons of this experience which seem to have wider significance. I am building mainly on the Polish experience, but many of the observations and propositions are relevant, *mutatis mutandis*, to other countries which have adopted a similar strategy.

II UTILISATION OF MANPOWER RESOURCES

The shaping of a development strategy is a dynamic process. Strategy has to change over time, follow a certain time-pattern, be adapted to changing conditions. Still, it seems possible to separate a certain 'package' of strategic solutions, relevant to a certain period of the development process. Most important is the period of the initial development acceleration. The strategy for this initial acceleration and for overcoming the inertia of underdevelopment has to concentrate primarily on two issues: first, the factors and forces that can set the economy and the society into new motion, breaking through the vicious circle of 'stagnant equilibrium'; second, engineering the development of feedbacks, reinforcing the process of change, making for the structural characteristics necessary for sustained development. I am particularly concerned here with the solution of the first issue.

The major strategic solution adopted for this objective in the socialist countries has consisted in using the available manpower resources to achieve development acceleration. I would not hesitate to call this strategic concept the great socio-economic innovation of socialism for overcoming economic underdevelopment. It was first applied in the Soviet Union, then in the socialist countries of Eastern Europe, then in China, and in a number of other socialist countries, in each case with certain specific features related to the socio-economic circumstances.

For Poland the following main considerations were at the background of the strategy of manpower utilisation:[1] first, the socialist principle of full employment; second, the availability of considerable underutilised manpower resources; third, the fact that this was the main available strategic instrument that could be used to give the economy an initial powerful 'push' towards development. I would not say that utilisation of labour resources for growth acceleration was conceived from the very beginning as a major strategic instrument. It took some time before its great strategic impact was fully recognised. Subsequently, the policy was to exploit it fully.

---

[1] This strategy was introduced at the beginning of the 1950s, and had its main impact during the first half of the 1950s. It was continued thereafter, though with diminishing effects.

In explaining the rationale of manpower utilisation strategy, as seen *ex post*, the following points merit attention:[2]

(1) New employment was channelled mainly to industry, construction and certain services, and it was these that were bringing immediate gains in the growth of output. Expansion of employment in those sectors was based on full utilisation of their capacities through increased shift-working, the operation of unprofitable and obsolete plants, and adopting labour-intensive technologies, particularly in construction work and in all auxiliary operations in industry.

(2) Additional manpower was drawn in ever increasing quantities from the rural population. It proved to be the main economic means of redistributing income in favour of the poorer sections of the population, and particularly in favour of the rural population.

(3) The economic proceeds of improved manpower utilisation were used to a considerable extent for capital accumulation. It is worth noting in this context that the distribution of those proceeds between consumption and accumulation was largely determined by the structure of capacity. The traditional economic choice – consumption versus savings – largely lost its relevance. This does not imply that the problem disappeared altogether; it took new forms, to recur again after the initial take-off in its traditional form.

(4) The great expansion of employment also had favourable effects on the development of skills, as well as on the morale of the nation.

Development experience has shown, however, that the strategy discussed also has certain dangers and drawbacks. For successful development it is necessary to be very careful about these dangers – to neutralise or minimise their occurrence in good time. Some lessons regarding this are presented below.

As has been said, the great expansion of employment had important consequences in the field of income distribution. The main impact is to be seen in the narrowing of the income gap between urban and rural population. This result was important in historical perspective not least from the point of view of social justice. It brought social and economic

---

[2] I shall not describe here the institutional conditions in which this strategy was applied; I take it for granted that they are known.

progress to a wide range of people who had come from the rural sector, and as a result the societal dynamism gained a new vigour. While the educational system facilitated their social advancement, at the basis of it were economic conditions which provided an equal start in life. These conditions were created by the employment and income distribution policies. While, however, these arguments were very well understood, and they formed the background of the employment and income distribution policies, practical experience brought certain unexpected complications. There appeared very quickly a complete restratification of the society in terms of income distribution patterns. Within only a few years the relative positions of different families and social groups in terms of incomes changed radically. This contributed to strong socio-political reactions against the policy.

A lesson can be drawn from this experience. It takes the form, in my view, of the necessity of very careful consideration of a society's capacity to absorb income distribution change. The required long-run trends of income distribution must be followed, but it is important not to exceed the capacity of a nation to absorb them. The study of capacity to absorb socio-economic change is, of course, a wider problem.

The policy of manpower utilisation that has been described was made easier by the introduction of a managerial system that permitted economic organisations to undertake a considerable expansion of employment. This radically changed the situation in the labour market. There developed a situation in which it was very 'easy to get a job'. This led to so-called social employment, to excessive labour mobility, and some other undesirable phenomena. All that had repercussions by weakening the motivations for good work. It is to be noticed that, while during the first stage of the manpower utilisation policy the positive effects of increased employment were most important, later on these negative aspects showed up strongly.

These difficulties were closely connected with the wider problem of the ways and means of implementing the manpower strategy. It is worthwhile to look more closely at experience in this field.

It is to be noted that increasing the labour input into traditional agriculture, or into construction of local infrastructure, may require social and institutional change. This, though it may prove difficult politically, nevertheless does not demand very sophisticated application. The same policy applied to industry may have a deep impact on the whole management system. Since in Poland the utilisation of the manpower resources took place mainly in industry, including construction, its implications for the management system were profound.

No sophisticated economic theory was developed to analyse the purpose of full manpower utilisation at the time when the policy was being introduced. It was taken for granted that people who work contribute to the national income, even if their productivity is low, while people who do not work contribute nothing and tend to become frustrated and demoralised. Still, two important problems remained to be answered: that of financing the new employment, and that of the type of economic system to be applied in economic institutions. Solutions of these two problems proved crucial and had far-reaching consequences. In commenting upon them I must present rather personal evaluations, since theoretical thinking on these and related problems has not as yet reached universal agreement.

In interpreting the actual policy it is worth noting that in planning the implementation of the development strategy not very much attention was given to the financial measures required. These measures were regarded as being of a rather secondary character in relation to such problems as institutional changes, the mobilisation of the forces for social development, the creation of new economic structures, and the like. Policy thinking was strongly influenced here by socialist ideology and Marxian theories. Two concepts were particularly relevant in this context. The first was a great emphasis on macroeconomic rationality. Rational solutions for the whole national economy were considered as completely dominating, while the functioning of any economic organisation had to be fully subordinated to these macro-policies. The second concept took the form of concentrating the development effort on two issues: guiding the social change and controlling the actual physical processes. Those constituted the main concern of development planning, while the financial flows and measures to implement them were considered as secondary and entirely instrumental.

These conceptual attitudes strongly influenced the practical economic solutions for implementing the manpower utilisation strategy. They consisted mainly in:

   (i) the generous financing of additional employment and of the costs of putting all available capacity into operation with public funds (the budget); to the extent that employment expansion did not produce proportionate increments in the supply of consumer goods and services, this policy resulted in price increases; thus this policy came to be considered as a mechanism by which the already employed financed the newly employed;

  (ii) creating an economic system for industrial organisations which would make possible an increased utilisation of manpower; this implied in particular the practical abandonment of profitability as a criterion of performance and wide application of subsidies covering high marginal costs resulting from additional employment and of full utilisation of capacity; it should be added that a system was created which also permitted additional employment in cases in which the marginal productivity of labour was lower than the marginal labour costs.

A third solution was added to those already mentioned:

(iii) a mechanism of market operation by which 'demand should exceed supply'; this was a mechanism attracting supply, and thus supporting a rapid quantitative growth of output; this, of course, necessitated the application of a firm control of prices.

These three solutions, together with certain other institutional and economic measures, formed a comprehensive socio-economic mechanism permitting and stimulating a large utilisation of manpower resources. The mechanism proved workable, though it also showed certain drawbacks, which became more and more visible with the advancement of the development process. It led to a great centralisation of decision-making; it failed to encourage efficiency at the firm level; it created obstacles to innovative dynamics; it led to a 'bad market'.[3]

This account of the experience, though inevitably greatly simplified, seems to allow the formulation of certain conclusions:

(1) The strategy of manpower utilisation as a means to faster and better progress proved workable in wide practical applications. The variety of countries in which it has been applied and the length of time for which it worked show that it is not to be regarded merely as a 'theoretical concept' only; it represents a real, tested alternative development process.
(2) The designing of this strategy and of its implementation may require a new approach in economic thinking. It would seem desirable that economic theories should incorporate this thinking into their conceptual framework.

---

[3] The instrumental solutions of the manpower utilisation strategy do not provide a full explanation of the indicated features; their reasons were more complex.

(3) The known solutions (of the kind described, for instance) should not necessarily be regarded as the perfect solutions; it seems possible to find different solutions, particularly with respect to practical measures of implementation.

III HUMAN MOTIVATIONS

Concentration of the development strategy on the human factor cannot be limited to the problem of manpower utilisation. While this may be a crucial issue during the initial period in countries starting an active development policy, other important problems arise. Let me turn again to the development experience of the socialist countries, concentrating on aspects which may have wider significance. It must be remembered however, that in discussing this experience we shall be concerned with the type of strategy which may be called 'growth-oriented'. This was the real strategy followed. And I assume that a great number of economically underdeveloped countries throughout the world would find this type of strategy desirable. In a 'growth-oriented' strategy particular attention is paid to those factors and forces which make for rapid progress in terms of physical output.

As has already been emphasised, there can be no economic development in the long run without the development of people. If one realises that, the question arises whether this justifies special policy measures in the field of human development. Most countries, both developing and developed, give a positive answer to that. This manifests itself particularly in educational and skill-promoting policies. This problem has received special emphasis in the development planning of the socialist countries. Though there are a number of important problems involved here, I shall not go into them, since they are widely appreciated.

Human development cannot be limited, however, to the raising of the skills and capabilities of people – technical, managerial, economic, and other. Another very important aspect arises, for which I use here the very wide notion of 'human motivation'. It appears with particular relevance in the context of a growth-oriented strategy.

Historical experience has shown that a policy aiming at a fast growth rate, promoted by means of employment and capital investment expansion, is likely to encounter a constraint in the human factor. If ignored, this may prove counterproductive with respect to the intended objective. It is thus possible that aiming directly at a high growth rate is not necessarily the best way of achieving it. This should be viewed, in my

.dgement, in the context of the interrelationships between the object-
es of the policy and human behaviour.

I advance the general proposition that right objectives of human
activities are a necessary condition of their efficacy. This is true not only
' simple activities but also of more complex activities with a wide social
ope. Erroneous, misguided objectives frustrate human behaviour. A
»ciety is integrated by a common sense of purpose, and this sense of
urpose strengthens the efficacy and rationality of human behaviour. If,
»wever, development objectives are not 'internalised' by the society, or
e not in accordance with the desires and expectations of the people, a
»nflict appears between the policy-objectives and the human be-
aviour; this must be expected to have a negative impact on the rate of
·ogress. The subordination of the development objectives to the needs
' the people can thus be seen to be a policy that increases overall
·ogress. I propose to call this interrelationship: *the basic motivational
·velopment feedback*. While I fully appreciate that the satisfaction of
e human needs is *per se* the right aim of development policy, I am
clined to stress that its pursuance only creates favourable conditions
»r faster progress. This general, somewhat philosophical, analysis may
: well exemplified from worldwide historical experience.

The recognition of the basic motivational development feedback is, to
y way of thinking, a common experience of the socialist countries, and
coming to be regarded as an important theoretical premise, though the
rminology may be different between country and country. It is not that
l the facts of a development policy can be interpreted in this way. It is,
»wever, a lesson of experience, widely understood and observed today.

In recent worldwide economic debates, strong arguments have been
»iced against the 'growth orientation' of development policy. So far as
e poor, developing countries are concerned, this argumentation seems
» be misdirected. What can and should be challenged is, to my thinking,
»t economic growth itself, but a specific pattern of growth which, in the
»ove terminology, ignores the basic motivational feedback. Thus one
:eds to consider the socio-economic relations making for a growth
attern which is socially irrelevant rather than challenge the desirability
' economic growth in those countries in which it does not satisfy the
asic needs of the people.

A development pattern subordinated to human needs creates the
asic conditions for the proper working of the human-motivations-
ipporting progress on the macro-societal scale. This, however, is far
om solving all the problems involving human motivation.

I am inclined to advance the proposition that the concentration of a

development strategy on the human factor makes it most important t
consider all the factors (socio-economic relations, policy objectives, an
the rest) which affect human motivation and thereby influence socic
economic progress. It should be observed, however, that this probler
does not seem to attract sufficient attention in economic thinking
Although in some theoretical work certain assumptions concernin
motivations may appear, explicitly or implicitly, the problem is nc
analysed thoroughly or systematically enough. This seems equally tru
of economic thinking in the socialist countries.

Motivation is a subject of interest in the management sciences. On
cannot, however, overlook the fact that almost all major questions c
development policy have a motivational implication. They shoulc
therefore, be subjected to economic analysis from this particular poin
of view. I would argue that any development strategy should be ver
carefully examined from the point of view of all its motivationa
implications.

In the socialist countries the problem of human motivation currentl
deserves particular attention. It has to be realised that socialism, for th
sake of certain important ideological premises, has weakened som
traditional forms of human motivation. By eliminating unemploymen
and pursuing a full employment policy, by developing a wide system o
social security, it has weakened those 'survival motivations' which fo
millenia have provided a moving force for human behaviour. It has als
rejected the motivations of a competitive market system. Putting
strong emphasis on social justice, it has at the same time diminished th
strength of individual self-interest. All those motivations need to b
replaced by other motivations, if the overall societal drive for progress i
not to be reduced.

While I do not intend to answer all the problems relating to th
socialist countries, or to the developing countries, I would emphasis
the necessity of attempting the analysis of all the factors that influenc
the human motivations contributing to socio-economic progress. Thi
problem area, largely neglected, deserves great attention.

IV HUMAN NEEDS

In the light of what has been said thus far, the human factor appear
mainly as a driving force in economic progress.[4] This is a justifiabl

---

[4] When using the term 'human factor' I have in mind also all the socio
economic relations which affect human behaviour.

approach in conditions in which societies are aiming at improving their efficiency and their living conditions. Those aims are valid and very important for a great number of the nations of the world, and for the developing nations particularly. For them, to stress that they can achieve faster and better progress if they properly rely on the human factor, is a legitimate strategic diagnosis.

It should, nonetheless, be observed that to do this implies a rather one-sided emphasis with regard to the interrelationships between the human beings and the development process; it should be noticed that the term 'human factor' itself suffers from this one-sidedness, since it treats human beings as a 'factor' in economic development. This emphasis came from the fact that we have been concerned mainly with experience of strategies of a 'growth-oriented' type. This orientation should not justify, however, neglect of other aspects of the interrelationship between human beings and the development process.

It has been widely realised in economic thinking that understanding of economic development in a narrow economic sense measured, for instance, by the increased volume of physical output, may lead to erroneous ideas and wrong strategies. Economic development is measured by what it implies for the people, and not by what it contributes to volumes of output or to financial flows. Dealing with such economic aggregates is unavoidable in economic thinking and development analysis. There is certainly nothing wrong with it, *per se*, if accompanied by a proper understanding of what it implies for the people. Strategy-making does not consist of manipulating these aggregate-variables, but of shaping the development patterns; and among the development patterns the most important are those which concern human beings and their social relations.

In considering what concerns human beings in the development process, two aspects can be usefully distinguished:

(i) human beings as the main agent of the development process, as a 'factor' in economic development;
(ii) human beings as recipients of the results of the development process.

This dichotomic division of the role of human beings in economic progress can be variously formulated. There is the familiar distinction of people as producers and of people as consumers. There is the familiar phrase 'development for the people and by the people'. In such and similar formulations this dichotomy is assumed, though depending upon the actual theoretical setting, it may have different meaning or different emphasis.

The conceptual dichotomy indicated may be useful if one does not ignore the important linkages between the two aspects concerned. I regard it as a way of organising one's argument. It follows that concepts which emphasise the role of the human factor as a driving force in economic progress need to be supplemented by concepts of human beings as recipients of the results, as consumers. This problem has many aspects. I find it convenient to discuss certain of them under the heading of 'human needs'.

It seems worth observing that the problem of human needs seems to be very much neglected in socio-economic thinking. It is really astonishing how little help many economic theories provide towards facing the problems of consumption and life-style patterns. In saying that I assume, of course, that these problems do exist, and that it is increasingly necessary to formulate and evaluate the strategic options in this respect. Some ten years ago this assumption would, perhaps, have been challenged by many. I would not expect that today, since the problem received a wide appreciation throughout the world.

There are many reasons why economic thinking is so irrelevant in the field of human needs and life-style patterns, and it would be interesting to consider them thoroughly. But I cannot tackle this problem in this paper. Let me attempt instead some more positive propositions.

Human needs and the ways of satisfying them can and should be considered on a macro-societal scale and in long-run terms. This is the theoretical approach which seems most promising, and within which strategic options can be formulated and evaluated. It is alien to the thinking of quite a number of theoretical schools, which seems to be the reason for their irrelevance to the field discussed. An approach to human needs from the individual's point of view, on the other hand, has not much to offer, in spite of all its sophistication.

Within a macro-societal, long-run approach to human needs and the ways of satisfying them, the following problems arise and deserve particular attention:

(1) *Interrelationships between life-style patterns and the ecological environment, seen in a long-term perspective.* Thinking along this line has developed recently in certain circles, and it has already produced important evidence and propositions, with strategic implications both for the whole of humanity and for particular nations.

(2) *Interrelationships between life-style patterns, particularly in rich countries, and the great economic disparities on the world scale.* While reasons for the existence of socio-economic discrepancies on the world scale represent a separate problem, there seems to be no doubt that life-style patterns are among the operating feedbacks here, and lead to further polarisation. There seem to be strong reasons to evaluate human needs patterns if their existence has global or international implications.

(3) *Interrelationships between life-style patterns and social relations within a society.* Needs and their satisfaction are not a purely 'individual affair' and societies may find it rational to evaluate their social implications and act accordingly.

(4) *The impact of the satisfaction of various human needs on the qualitative features of the human beings – physical, intellectual and cultural.* It is fashionable in certain schools of economic thinking to reject the so-called 'arbitrary' evaluation of human needs; they too readily ignore the manipulation of human needs by business, advancing strong arguments against the right of public authorities to interfere with the consumption pattern. In general, however, a readiness to attempt evaluation of human needs seems to be developing in socio-economic thinking. This is the right line, in my view, though it requires adequate theoretical foundation.

In traditional economic thinking human needs have been understood and classified in terms of what has been 'traded' – needs concerned with economic goods and services having use-value. This concept has served economic thinking not at all badly as far as the basic, biological needs have been concerned. Human needs cannot be limited, however, to this category of needs only. People have needs for expression, for creativity, for involvement, for justice, for harmony and beauty, and so on. Should these be of concern to socio-economic thinking? I have no doubts about this. Let me consider a few related problems.

In recent years, the theory of 'basic needs' has been advanced in certain circles, with strategic implications in the context of international relations. This theory has marked a departure from traditional 'market theories', since it has assumed both evaluation of consumption patterns and interference with them. It is astonishing, however, how little theoretical thinking has gone into this concept. A 'basic needs' concept should surely imply that the remaining needs are in some sense 'secondary', that the primary needs should have priority in the time-sequence of the development process. Can this be defended in the light of the wide historical experience of human civilisation? I have serious doubts about it. Human beings have never limited themselves, even during the very early and 'primitive' stages of civilisation, to biological needs alone. This has been because people have never been biological organisms only; they have been human beings, and have always had specific needs arising from their human nature. Without those needs, civilisation would not have come about. These specific human needs, additional to the biological ones, are in the same way at the very roots of the civilisation progress today for all nations, and thus they cannot be ignored. This does not imply that the theory of basic needs has no merits. It is certainly right in emphasising that the full range of social strata should always benefit from the development process. Its relevance might, however, be much improved if it were based on a wider analysis of human needs.

The history of humanity seems to show that such needs as that for expression, for creativity, for involvement, for justice, for harmony and beauty, are the great human needs which have been the engine of human culture and civilisation. If those needs are ignored or neglected, because of certain features in the working of economic systems, there arises dissatisfaction, anxiety, alienation, with a negative impact on human motivations and capabilities. A great part of the dissatisfaction, anxiety and frustration, which seems to characterise certain sections of the contemporary society, may perhaps be attributed to a neglect of those needs? I do not think that we can give a quite definite answer to that question, but it seems important to keep it in mind all the time.

V SOME CONCLUSIONS

In conclusion, I see strong reasons why socio-economic thinking should include the consideration of human needs. It is in this field that the most important feedbacks from human beings to the development process appear. They have the most critical consequences for the future of mankind.

In presenting the foregoing ideas I have deliberately put the main emphasis on the humanistic approach to development problems. It is not that this approach explains all the mechanisms of the development process. But it is very important and very productive. This can, I believe, be seen not only in the light of the arguments that I have presented but also in the light of actual experience. Not all the relevant problems have been covered, it is true, and more questions have been asked than answered. I hope that this will be appreciated.

I hope that during this congress there will be discussion in particular of the ways and means of utilising manpower in the conditions that prevail in the developing countries, of the 'motivational approach' to development strategies, and of the conceptual assumptions in considering the problems of human needs.

Comments on Dr Pajestka's Paper: 'Basing Development Strategy on the Human Factor'[1]

P. Maillet

France

1 THE ECONOMY MUST BE ORGANISED FOR THE PEOPLE

This is the fundamental principle which informs the whole of Józef Pajestka's paper, and I applaud it. I also like the emphasis he places on the idea of a strategy for development. This is a problem that is not limited to the developing countries alone, for no country is as developed as it would like to be.

But the subject is so vast that the author inevitably dealt less fully with some points than with others. I would like to amplify a few points that he has merely alluded to and to add further arguments to some others which require more searching study.

Three fundamental questions dominate every attempt at devising and applying a strategy for development. These are:

(1) *What do people want*? What is the scale of their concerns and their aims?
(2) *What can people do*? What, for any given country at any given time, is its room for manoeuvre, its range of possible alternative development patterns?
(3) *How can people be induced to act in such a manner as to maximise the achievement of attainable aims*? That is the problem of organising the economic system and relations between countries.

2 WHAT DO PEOPLE WANT?

Józef Pajestka declares himself to be astonished that the problem of human needs has been so neglected in socio-economic thinking. I do not fully share this point of view. It is true that economic theory gives us no arguments by which to grade human needs in practice. But is this so astonishing? The determination of human needs is a matter not of economics, but of philosophy and politics. The problem is not how to draw up a catalogue of needs on the basis of some theoretical proposition, but how to create mechanisms and procedures for identifying individual needs in the light of the overall aspirations of all the

---

[1] Translated by Elizabeth Henderson

members of a country's population. This is the essence of democracy. It is only thereafter that the economist has a part to play by recommending ways and means of coming as close as possible to the satisfaction of these aspirations or by suggesting certain well-defined and more or less quantified targets by which these can be translated into practice.

In this connection I wish to draw attention to a passage in Pajestka's paper which could easily be misinterpreted, namely, when he writes (p. 16) that 'human needs and the ways of satisfying them can and should be looked upon in a macro-societal scale', and that the 'approach to human needs from the individual's point of view . . . has not much to offer in spite of all its sophistication'. If this is meant as a criticism of certain mathematical excesses in the neo-classical approach, I agree wholeheartedly. Nor am I alone in doing so. Let me recall a remark of the great econometrician Ragnar Frisch at the first World Econometric Congress: 'All that is playometrics'. And centuries ago Aristotle declared that man is fundamentally a sociable creature. But society is there to help men prosper, and not the other way round. It follows that several different types of society are possible and admissible provided they leave men free to express all their generous aspirations. Anything that involves the risk of dictatorship, on the part of an individual, of a single political party or of a plutocratic oligarchy, is not compatible with observance of the variety of relative priorities assigned by different individuals to different needs – including 'needs of expression, of creativity, of participation, of justice, of harmony and beauty', as Pajestka rightly points out (p. 17).

Even though such considerations may be at the frontier of economics, they are of fundamental importance for the subject under discussion here. But there is another subject which falls fully within the purview of this congress, namely, how to use the fruits of economic progress to enhance human resources. It is my hope that on such questions as the amount of spending on education, health, cultural activities and research the coming debates this week will preserve a fair balance between two aspects of expenditure: expenditure with a view to improving the factor of production of man, and expenditure with a view to making the economy's productive potential enhance the condition of man. In so doing, we shall correct a defect of economic literature, which often tends to give more weight to the first aspect than to the second. Comparisons between different countries should prove fruitful in this respect, from the point of view not of setting a standard, but of making us give more thought to the use to be made of productive potentials which, even in countries we call developed, are always limited.

3 THE SECOND QUESTION: WHAT CAN PEOPLE DO?

Józef Pajestka argues (pp. 4–5) 'that the development process is not historically predetermined but that it can be influenced'. In other words, the course of history is not traced in advance, and man remains master of his destiny. This belief in the possibility of man's freedom of action certainly deserves forceful reaffirmation because it underlies all our endeavours to improve economic and social development. But without denying this possibility, we must yet ask ourselves how much room for manoeuvre any particular country actually has in this fourth quarter of the twentieth century.

The question is all the more worth raising as we observe that both superpowers encounter great obstacles to developing as they want, in so far as both have to rely on imports from abroad, in the one case of a sizable part of energy supplies and in the other of technology and to some extent grains. *A fortiori*, the development of smaller countries is subject to many constraints.

But while it would be patently wrong for any country to assume that its development must inexorably follow a path previously traversed by other (supposedly more advanced) countries and that it must conform to a ready-made model, it would be equally wrong to believe that just any development pattern is possible at all times. Geographical restrictions are often severe, the legacy of history is heavy, the constraints deriving from economic relations with the rest of the world may be very restrictive. These latter are of particular relevance to a meeting of economists from all over the world. Let me recall three of them.

In the case of some countries, and most often the poorest, some 70 or 80 per cent of export earnings come from just one, two, or at most three products. The maintenance and, if possible, the increase of its export earnings is of crucial importance to such a country, and so is the stability of their purchasing power. These aims are all the more difficult to achieve as the commodities in question are often of the kind for which demand grows slowly, or for which there are substitutes. We discussed these problems three years ago, in Tokyo.

Energy production is concentrated in a few countries. More than half the energy products moving through international trade come from the Middle East. Hence the development of any country, rich or poor, without energy resources of its own largely depends upon the strategies adopted by that tiny part of the world.

Finally, almost 40 per cent of the world's scientific and technological research is done in the United States. Moreover, one of the two other great producers of research, Western Europe, fashions its programmes largely upon American models, and the third, the Soviet Union, buys western technology on a large scale. The great bulk of today's research in the world, and with it the direction of tomorrow's technological progress for a quarter of a century to come, is shaped to fit the scale of values of one single country – and one which accounts for no more than 5 per cent of world population.

This is a matter of the utmost seriousness, and it is a pity that it does not figure explicitly on the agenda of the congress; yet it can be discerned in the programme of several special sessions and it is to be hoped that it will be discussed fully.

4 HOW TO ACHIEVE THE OBJECTIVES PEOPLE DESIRE

This is the problem of motivation, to which Pajestka devotes much space. It is also the problem of choice of an economic system. In this connection I should like to place the most vigorous stress on the variety of possible types of development, and on the advantage of preserving that variety in the interests of mankind as a whole.

The world has room for many different development patterns, each corresponding to a particular people's genius. I think I am in agreement with one of the ideas implicit in Pajestka's macro-societal approach when I say that nations are realities which must not be ignored and that they are of value to the extent that they are distinguished not by opposition one to the other, but by exalting a certain set of values and exemplifying a certain life-style. The existence of these diversities is one of mankind's riches and it must be carefully preserved, for it is much easier to destroy than to recreate.

What are the consequences of this state of affairs for us as economists? I can name two. First and foremost, we must give up the idea of a single development model and a single economic system to be propagated all over the world. The North has rendered signal service to the South by passing on to it technical know-how, but it has also handicapped the South by offering, and sometimes imposing upon it, ready-made models, however valid these may appear to be in the view of one or the other of the northern nations. The South has to work out its own models – as, speaking for his own continent, the African historian Ki-Zerbo puts it: 'We need a positive ideology encompassing the various aspects of individual and social life in one overall design, not a mere mechanical repetition of outside lessons learnt by rote'.[2]

[2] Joseph Ki-Zerbo, *Histoire de l'Afrique Noire* (Paris, Hatier, 1978).

Similarly, the Indian philosopher Claude Alvares[3] writes that genuine development resides within each ethno-cultural system and not in the adoption or imitation of some dominant paradigm imported from outside. What we have to do is to reconcile the autonomy of each system with its integration into a setting of interrelations based upon common acceptance of different values.

In the short run, it is obviously more difficult to think out and put into effect original models than to copy some existing one, but in the medium and long run they are likely to be much more promising. But time presses: in twenty years it will probably be too late.

The second consequence for us as economists is that we need to give much more thought to the organisation of international trade. We have, on the one hand, the formula of undiluted free trade, which often brings more benefits to the rich than to the poor, and may create unexpected disturbances in the production, and hence employment, of some of the trading partners, which may present great obstacles to a development plan reflecting national priorities, and which therefore stands in danger of self-destruction by its own excesses, in so far as it may cause a groundswell of protectionist reaction. On the other hand, we have a system whose dominant aim is autarky, where foreign trade is regarded as a mere appendage of national activity, something to be called upon only for absolutely unavoidable imports – in short, a system prepared to forgo the reciprocal gains from trade among nations. But between these two patterns it must be possible to devise a third, by organising interdependence without exacerbating dependence. The programme of our congress opens the prospect of important contributions to this subject, even though it will need another World Congress before the world community of economists can fully meet this challenge.

[3] Claude Alvares, *Homo Faber: Technology and Culture in India, China and the West from 1500 to the Present Day* (The Hague, Nijhoff, 1980).

Comments on Dr Pajestka's Paper: 'Basing Development Strategy on the Human Factor'

Armando Labra
Mexico

I must thank the organising committee for giving me the opportunity to comment on the work of such a distinguished authority as Dr Józef Pajestka, whose work has contributed greatly over the past twenty years to the development of economic, political and social theory, always discovering new answers to the pressing needs.

I welcome also the opportunity of sharing this discussion with a distinguished disciple of two economists who, like himself, have contributed to raise the social and political levels of economic thought. I have in mind particularly Oscar Lange and Mikal Kalecki.

I would like to stress some of the most important points in Dr Pajestka's suggestive and valuable paper, so that it remains in our minds throughout the congress. I believe that everybody would agree with the feeling of dissatisfaction that runs through Dr Pajestka's paper, and is shared by many other social and economic thinkers, regarding the lack of success of economic theory and other studies in achieving a development theory that is concerned with the betterment of human welfare in all its aspects. In fact, unemployment and social deprivation are the most important features of the living standards of the vast majority of the world population.

It would be hard to find an economist who can honestly deny that his theoretical thinking in some measure fails to answer to the essential purpose of all scientific work: human welfare and the political and ideological commitments to achieve it. In his lucid presentation Dr Pajestka reminds us of this obvious fact, which has been a permanent matter of concern for many of us. But Dr Pajestka suggests practical ways of progressing towards the theoretical design of a new concept that will grasp the great forgotten political and social objective, the heart of our discipline.

Pajestka treats the contents of a development strategy, not as strictly economic issues but, more properly, as political and social issues, adopting a scheme of analysis described as a global perspective, which I consider fundamental. I would also consider essential his concept of the dynamic nature of the development process, which needs to be formulated in a long-term perspective. And, what I consider most important about his argument: that the development strategy must be conceived as a social phenomenon closely related to real political issues.

If we concentrate on this last point, it will be easy to see why the

treatment of the human factor as the ultimate purpose of the develop
ment process has not hitherto been a dominant feature in economi
theory and policy. On the contrary, as a result of the systematic pursui
of attempts to depoliticise and technocratise economic thought, w
might imagine that the objective and strategic aim of development is not
nor ever will be, mankind.

Many participants in this congress will agree with the urgent need t
develop a new approach in economic thought that focuses on th
internal sources of development, and regard this as essential fo
achieving the welfare levels that the vast majority of the worl
population demands. Thus, Pajestka's proposal seems fundamental i
that it makes it clear that economic development must be subordinate
to the priorities of social interest. To this social content, all economi
changes must be adjusted and, to achieve its objectives, political force
must when necessary be employed, leaving economic and administrativ
measures to their instrumental functions. We have been doing th
opposite. The consequences are to be seen in the form of a worldwid
economic crisis and social and political decline threatening in th
majority of countries.

A highlight of Pajestka's argument is that it restores, in theoretica
and practical terms derived from the Polish experience, the idea o
treating human resources as the primary objective and simultaneousl
as the practical instrument of economic policy for the achievement o
development. As he rightly says, this is the great socio-economi
innovation of socialism.

The author describes the experience of his country, Poland, and i
doing so both presents the historical evidence and encourages us t
accept political and theoretical reasoning which in practice provides
strategy for human resources that will accelerate and improve progres
and is based on practical experience; at the same time it helps us t
overcome the difficulties that already confront us and to design new
policies suitable to the particular characteristics of our regions.

As to making the human factor both the objective and the means o
achieving the development strategy, the real state of the politica
economy and of economic policy show how different have been th
priorities in developing countries, such as Mexico and most of the Third
World, where the most evident results have been inflation, under
employment, unemployment and insufficient food supply, under th
influence of the pressures of expansion in the industrialised economies

This point has become of immense importance since, withou
question, there has been interruption of the attempts to develop many o

he peripheral countries resulting from repeated imposition of econ-
mies and pragmatic short-term policy measures, in spite of their very
onsiderable social and economic effects. The overriding influence of
hort-term considerations on decisions, conceived only in terms of
uantitative production targets or financial results, has in practice
ubordinated social welfare to monetary indicators.

Dr Pajestka explores that fascinating topic, human motivations. The
arious historical experiences in socialist and non-socialist countries
how that, despite achieving high levels of social welfare and employ-
1ent, people's essential motivations may weaken and, in some cases,
ven disappear. Many forms of motivation have been operating for
housands of years, actually determining human behaviour, as the
uthor points out.

Another relevant matter of concern is that experience in socialist
ountries of diminishing the individual incentives derived from com-
etition has created a vacuum that still requires to be filled by means of a
ompletely changed motivational concept that is consistent with social
eeds and that can effectively replace those now being superseded. This
oint is of basic concern for peripheral countries engaged in integrating
opular activity by motivating it in accord with an integral perspective
equired by the strategy of development. If, as Pajestka suggests,
:conomic development has significance in what it implies to the people,
nd not in what it brings in terms of production or financial flows', in
ountries like ours we must then make a tremendous effort to establish
1e human factor as the genuine recipient of the results of development.
'his requires, above all else, re-examination of the historical concept of
uman needs in specific societies, and then the creation of a viable
cheme of social motivations, finally nourishing it politically through
he support of the popular sectors.

It is here that Pajestka sets a great challenge, but also raises great
oubt. In his conception of human needs, covering not only biological
eeds, but also those qualitatively identified with man's fullest contri-
ution to civilisation and culture, such as liberty, justice, involvement,
eauty, and the rest, he states a purpose, but leaves us with the
1junction to build a conceptual bridge that will link human needs with
ocial motivations so that both become a drive for social, economic and
olitical order as well as instruments in a development strategy based on
1e human factor.

It is clear that human needs must be satisfied within a macro-social
erspective, considered in long-run terms and that to neglect this aspect
nd its theorical implications, must make any theory irrelevant. Thus

the absence of a conceptual bridge, between needs and the concrete forms of a social motivational scheme for a strategy like the one proposed, prevents the working out of the author's thesis. This is the case in relation to life-styles, seen from the ecological and long-run point of view; it is the case for the contrasts between rich and poor countries and it is the case for the conflicts within a society that oppose the individual to the scheme of social needs.

The problem becomes yet more complex when one tries to measure human needs at an intellectual, sophisticated and highly qualitative level; but above all, when one deals with basic human needs that are not necessarily derived from specific historical conditions and where analysis opens a wide range of philosophical and political consider ations.

The lack of such a bridge also explains the question posed by the author when he suggests that one must abandon the concept of 'basic needs' as a simple end product of the development task. It is evident that this issue must be an intellectual responsibility belonging to specific societies or particular regional interests.

With this in mind, I would like to return to Dr Pajestka's proposals and make one of my own: without claiming too much, I feel obliged to say that it seems to me that any contribution to building the bridge needed to integrate human needs with a social motivational scheme that will support a development strategy for popular welfare, must have its starting point in an essentially political consideration. In effect, history shows that if the ideological and political component that integrates any society in a shared, clear and united purpose is lacking, popular motivisation to achieve in practice any sort of democratic and independent development strategy becomes unlikely.

It seems that the prime task, the economists' first responsibility – like that of anybody who has an overall vision of development – is to discover forms of political organisation that can rally popular support and to exercise pressure upon the authorities to design a development strategy related to collective welfare and human needs. In Pajestka's terms, I think that should be the fundamental macro-motivation issue

In the countries in the capitalist periphery it also seems unlikely that the power systems will graciously accept the revision and reformulation of the objectives and strategies of development, because their rationality responds to individual motivations that are embodied in the dominant accumulation processes of the capitalist system. Thus, it becomes imperative to employ the pressure that an independent and organised working class can impose upon public power decisions as the most important vehicle of change towards the new strategy. There is no other social force that can propose and implement a change of the *status quo*, which is, by the way, quite alien to the social purposes that Pajestka judiciously suggests.

With realism, Professor Pajestka accepts the necessity of making an exercise to introduce real politics into these proposals regarding economic issues. Let us do it then. Let us accept this suggestion in this congress and restore the essentials: the human objectives of development that, as is obvious, have increasingly been displaced by minor concerns about a point more, a point less, in the rate of inflation, about the exchange rate, or about the increase in manufacturing production, to disregard the real issues.

Let us hope that this congress may give an impulse to eliminate technocratic imagery, alien to society and politics. With Pajestka's suggestions, we may become better able to combine an economic, political and social vision of development with scientific rigour, taking into account the overwhelming failure of economics to cope, without the assistance of other disciplines, with the task of the full development of the human being, urgently required by the largest part of deprived, starved and diseased humanity, and forgotten by the theoreticians of economic efficiency.

2 The Latin-American Periphery in the Global System of Capitalism[1]

Raul Prebisch

ARGENTINA AND UNITED NATIONS

I A BRIEF OVERVIEW

THE DYNAMICS OF THE CENTRES

The exclusive and conflictive development of the periphery evolved within a world context of capitalism under the hegemony of the centres and, more especially, of its major centre. Historically, the dynamic role has fallen to the centres while the periphery has taken a subsidiary role in the spontaneous development of capitalism.

The term 'subsidiary role' is used in the sense that although the dynamic of the centres has been, and continues to be, important to the periphery, it is far from sufficient. In fact, in this case, technological progress and its fruits have tended to be concentrated in the centres themselves. Furthermore, industrialisation and the trade of industrial goods prompted by the incessant diversification of the former are also concentrated in the centres. Thus, capitalism proves to be essentially centripetal.

The advanced countries in which capitalism evolves – the centres –

[1] This is a résumé of the principal ideas contained in papers published by the author in CEPAL magazine: 'Criticism of Capitalism on the Periphery' (No. 1, 1st semester 1976); 'Socio-economic Structure and the Crisis of the System' (No. 6, second semester 1978); 'The Neoclassic Theories of Economic Liberalism' (No. 7, April 1979); 'Towards a Transformation Theory' (to be published in CEPAL magazine No. 10, April 1980).

tend to spread the dynamic of their development to others – the periphery – except to the extent needed to ensure the centres their supplies of primary products. Therefore the periphery tended to remain on the fringes of the industrialising process during the historical development of capitalism and later, when the periphery in turn industrialised, it was divorced from the centres' major flows of trade, where this process manifested itself. Thus this peculiar dynamic of the centres tended to limit the scope of development on the periphery, in conjunction with other internal factors.

On the other hand, the centres propagated their technical expertise, patterns of consumption and life-styles, institutions, ideas and ideology to the periphery. Thus capitalism on the periphery proved to be essentially imitative.

During this century, two major crises have occurred in the centres which have had far-reaching repercussions on the periphery. Institutions failed to adapt fully to the changing demands made by this dynamic process, to the enormous development of technology and its ambivalence and to the play of power politics, which have had such a marked effect on the distribution of the fruits of technology.

THE TWO MAJOR CRISES OF CAPITALISM

The first crisis to occur in the major dynamic centre of capitalism was embodied in the depression of the 1930s. As a result, the already limited development of the periphery was sharply cut back and inward industrialisation imposed. In spite of its defects, this substitutive industrialisation allowed the periphery to grow at a rate which exceeded that of its inadequate exports to the centres.

The second great crisis is that in the throes of which capitalism today finds itself. During the centres' long years of euphoria preceding the crisis, the periphery began to boost industrialisation towards the exterior. This became increasingly necessary as the policy of substitution came closer to exhaustion. The export of industrial goods was boosted, especially in those countries in which industrialisation had made the greatest strides in the preceding phase, during which it had been directed inwards. However, it is evident that even this second crisis has failed to dispel the centripetal tendency of capitalism.

Thus the external brake on development of the periphery has once more been applied. The centres have not particularly favoured industrial trade with the periphery and neither has the latter taken full advantage of the extensive possibilities at its disposal for reciprocal trade, as the centres did among themselves.

THE IMITATIVE CAPITALISM OF THE PERIPHERY

This phenomenon of the propagation exercised by the centres has always occurred in the periphery. However, it becomes more marked with increasing industrialisation. Thus the imitative capitalism of the periphery is based on the characteristics of the centres to an ever greater extent, attempting to develop in their image and likeness within a social structure which is very different from their own.

The strategy of growing productivity common to the centres has become increasingly widespread. But its fruits are wasted on account of excessive imitation of the centres' patterns of consumption, as promoted by the mass media. This, together with the centres' siphoning off of income, occurs at the expense of a capital accumulation which is essential if large sectors of the population are to be absorbed and increasing productivity maintained. This explains the exclusive nature of capitalism in internal development on the periphery, which is further emphasised by exceptional demographic growth. The latter is yet another consequence of the propagation of methods which protect and prolong the human life span.

This imitation of the centres' patterns of consumption is especially notable in the upper brackets of the social structure which constitute the privileged consumer society.

THE SURPLUS AND THE CRISIS OF CAPITALISM ON THE PERIPHERY

These groups appropriate the greater part of the fruits of technological progress, that is, the economic surplus. This phenomenon is, in fact, inherent in capitalism. However, on the periphery, it appears with specific features. Namely, the transfer of the institutional regime of appropriation to the periphery occurs within a heterogeneous social structure opposed to the distribution of the benefits of technological progress to the greater part of the labour force. This is a consequence of the laws of the market.

Nevertheless, the structural mutations inherent in development incur increasing pressures aimed at sharing the surplus in the ambit both of the market and of the state. These pressures and the phenomenon of surplus appropriation are the expression of changing power relations and are not subject to any regulatory principle. As these pressures become more pronounced thanks to the effective operation of democratic institutions (effective as opposed to merely nominal) they tend to draw the system into a crisis.

That is to say, an internal crisis of capitalism on the periphery, which also extends to its relationships with the centres. The centres seek to promote this imitative form of capitalism, which excludes large sectors of the population from development, for all they are worth, and conflict consequently arises on account of these pressures to share out the surplus. This is a form of capitalism suffering from many internal contradictions, to which external contradictions are added in centre–periphery relations. In the latter case, there are two principal contradictions. Firstly, the contradiction between the increasing tendency to internationalise consumption and the precarious internationalisation of its production towards the periphery. And, secondly, the old contradiction resulting from the hegemony of the centres, between new manifestations of dependence added to those which already existed and the increasing sense of autonomy which is inherent in development.

The above factors further complicate the already difficult transformation of development on the periphery, where this transformation seeks to reconcile the vitality of development, social equality and the democratisation process and, furthermore, to consecrate the authenticity of such development. However, these aims cannot be achieved while conventional theories built up in the centres continue to predominate. Nor could such development be based on anti-capitalist theories, whatever the validity of certain of their arguments.

Thus this necessary and fundamental transformation is a largely unknown quantity, in political terms. In vain will the centres attempt to seek to avoid it with their ideological harangues. Their exaltation of imitative capitalism lacks foresight. This element of long-term vision is also absent in capitalism on the periphery. The right road has not yet been found and valuable time has been lost.

II THE INTERNAL DYNAMICS OF CAPITALISM ON THE PERIPHERY

MUTATIONS IN SOCIAL STRUCTURE

The imitative development of the periphery is characterised by persistent phenomena involving the centres' propagation of their technology, patterns of consumption and other modes of cultural behaviour,

institutions, ideas and ideologies. The above factors develop belatedly in
a social structure which differs substantially from the social structure
which has evolved in the centres. This gives rise to major internal
contradictions in development on the periphery and also to external
contradictions related to the centripetal nature of developed capitalism.

Technology penetrates through the accumulation of capital both in
physical terms and in the training of human resources. As this process
evolves, continual changes occur in the social structure. This structure
embraces a series of partial structures linked by close relationships of
interdependence, namely technological, industrial and occupational
structures and also the structure of power.

The penetration of the centres' productive technology occurs by
means of successive levels of increasing productivity and efficacy
superimposed on previous levels of lower productivity and efficacy,
while pre-capitalist or semi-capitalist levels continue to exist at the
bottom of this technological structure.

THE STRUCTURAL SURPLUS

These changes in technological structure go hand in hand with changes
in the structure of employment. Labour is continually moving from the
lowest levels of productivity to higher productivity levels. However, in
the play of market forces, the remuneration of most of the labour force is
not increased in correlation with this increased productivity. This can be
explained by the regressive competitiveness of labour employed in low
productivity sectors or of the unemployed. Only a part of the fruits of
technological progress is transferred to a small portion of the labour
force which has been able to acquire the increasingly demanding
qualifications required by technology, principally on account of social
standing.

That portion of the benefits of growing productivity which is not
transferred to the labour force is the surplus which is appropriated
mainly by the upper-income brackets where the greater part of capital in
physical goods and land-ownership is concentrated. There is no
tendency for the surplus to disappear in competition between
companies – even if this were free of restrictions – nor in a drop in price.
The surplus is, rather, retained by the companies as a result of the
monetary expansion accompanying the productive process, as will be
seen below.

THE EXCLUSIVE AND CONFLICTING TENDENCIES OF THE SYSTEM

This unequal income distribution in favour of the upper-income brackets leads them to imitate the centres' patterns of consumption. This type of behaviour by the privileged consumer society implies a considerable wastage in capital accumulation potential. Nor is this wastage apparent only in the amount of capital, but also in its composition. In fact, the expansion of productivity and income through technology leads to the use of combined techniques for the purpose of continually diversifying the production of goods and services. This change in the productive structure brings about a rise in the proportion of consumption capital, which does not increase productivity, at the expense of the reproductive capital needed to boost development. This phenomenon is accentuated by other forms of consumption capital accumulation, both in the public and private sectors.

This phenomenon is inherent in the development dialectics of the centres but has occurred prematurely in the periphery, due to widespread distributive inequality.

A further factor hindering accumulation is the centres' siphoning off of income, especially through transnational corporations. This is made possible by their technological and economic superiority and hegemonic power.

This inadequate and frustrated accumulation of reproductive capital and exceptional demographic growth are the main reasons for the system's inability fully to absorb the lower strata of the social structure and to tackle other expressions of excess labour. This is the exclusive tendency of the system.

Those falling within these strata are most numerous in agriculture. Since there is very little diversification in demand for agricultural goods, labour is inclined to move to other activities. However, because the system does not have sufficient absorption capacity, extensive redundancy occurs, which accounts for the relative deterioration of agricultural labour income. While the system fails to correct this insufficient absorbency, progress in agriculture will not serve either to increase income in this area or correct its relative deterioration. Rather, when production exceeds demand a deterioration in relative prices ensues. This tendency occurs above all in the case of agricultural exports, consequently braking expansion in this field which, in turn, exercises an adverse effect on development.

As technology penetrates the social structure, certain changes occur which are reflected in the structure of power. The middle classes grow and, as the democratisation process advances, their power is augmented, thereby presenting an ever stronger challenge to that of the upper-income groups, where most of the means of production are concentrated. These power relations exist in both the market and state spheres.

In the market sphere, the middle groups bring their labour union pressure to bear to ensure their share of the surplus and in defence of what they have already won for themselves. In the state sphere, they use their political power to obtain social services and increases in employment. Thus, the state generally becomes an agent of spurious labour absorption. To this end, the state acquires a part of the surplus, as well as fulfilling its civil and military functions in the acquisition of goods and services in the market.

The double pressure which is exerted on the surplus leads the middle classes to imitate the centres' patterns of consumption although, of course, to a much lesser extent than the upper-income groups. The structural distribution thus becomes, fundamentally, a play of power relations although, of course, individual differences in capacity and dynamism also have their effect.

On account of the surplus and the capital which can thereby be accumulated, the upper-income groups hold the dynamic key to the system. This functions acceptably while the surplus continues to mount as a result of successive productivity increases, in spite of the double pressure on sharing referred to above. As this process is not subject to any regulatory principles, any sharp intensification of this pressure and the ensuing capture of successive productivity increases at the expense of surplus increase leads to a weakening in accumulation and affects the behaviour of the privileged consumer society. This gives rise to the conflictive phenomena of the system since companies react by raising prices in order to restore the dynamic of the surplus. This chain reaction becomes increasingly disturbing in that, following this reaction by companies, labour in turn counterreacts during the democratisation process. This is how an inflationary spiral of a social nature originates and develops. This aggravation of the distributive struggle limits the system's capacity for absorbing the growing labour force, which consequently vegetates in the lower brackets.

THE CRISIS OF THE SYSTEM

This is the nature of the crisis within the system in the advanced stages of development when the play of power relations gathers momentum. This phenomenon occurs in the advanced stages of development on the periphery. This is not the case in countries where the democratisation process is incipient and does not genuinely develop; that is, where it is apparent as opposed to real democracy. The system's tendency towards this crisis can be postponed for a relatively long period in cases where large funds arising from the exploitation of a non-renewable natural resource are available.

The political power of the upper-income brackets, which had seemed to decline with the advance of democracy, gains a new foothold as a result of the upheaval through which the inflationary crisis of the system makes itself apparent. Force is then brought to bear in order to break the labour unions and political power held by underprivileged groups.

If military power is not necessarily under the economic and political control of the upper classes, it would not be unreasonable to question the motives for their intervention in the service of the privileged consumer society. This, undeniably, involves a complicated interplay of factors. The explanation resides basically in the fact that since the upper brackets hold the dynamic key to such a system, that is, the capital-accumulation capacity, a laissez-faire policy is established in their efforts to restore the regularity of development. But this is achieved only at an enormous social, as well as political, cost. This, in fact, constitutes the end of democratic liberalism but it often occurs that ideas of economic liberalism flourish at the same time – an adulterated liberalism which, far from ensuring the sharing out of the fruits of development, flagrantly consolidates social inequity.

As yet, none of the attempts made to establish democratic liberalism in Latin America has been successful. We are already too familiar with its vicissitudes, its promising advances and distressing retreats. But not all can be explained by past experience. New and complex factors arise as changes occur in the social structure. And the use of force has acquired a new meaning which is very different from in the past. Namely, that of completely divorcing democratic liberalism and economic liberalism, in spite of the fact that both grew from the same philosophical roots.

THE RETENTION OF THE SURPLUS AND THE VULNERABILITY OF THE SYSTEM

The importance of the above points suggests that a detailed explanation should be given of the manner in which the dynamic key to the system functions. The dynamic need continually to augment the surplus and reproductive accumulation could not be fulfilled if increased productivity led to a drop in prices. That is not how capitalism works. This drop in prices can only be avoided if demand increases to an extent which is at least sufficient to absorb the level of supply resulting from the growth in productivity. This dictates that income paid by companies to the factors of production, which is where demand originates, should be higher than the income contained in the cost of the supply of final goods. Thus, when these final goods are sold in the market, companies recover the incomes paid to produce them as well as the higher incomes allowing the benefits of productivity to be absorbed without resulting in a drop in prices. These higher incomes return to the companies in the form of a surplus and are incorporated into the demand.

Where do these higher incomes originate? The answer lies in the existence of a dynamic phenomenon. The growth of final production in addition to the increase in fixed capital (which we will omit for the purposes of simplification) requires that production be increased ahead of the final goods, which do not appear until some time later. For this reason, companies direct income from those areas which absorb the final supply. In fact, the incomes thereby paid to the factors of production in successive stages of the process are higher than those contained in the final supply. This growing mass of income counterbalances the circulating capital constituted by the production in progress. If these incomes are thus higher than those required to prevent prices from dropping, why does the reverse not occur?

The explanation is very simple. Only a part of such incomes is immediately translated into demand for finished goods. A further portion is directed towards demand for services, both in the market and the state sphere, circulates there and gradually returns as demand for goods.

Besides the income paid to the factors of production, companies acquire imported goods and thus the countries from which these goods originate recover the incomes paid out during production as well as the corresponding surplus. The reverse occurs in the case of exports.

There is no strict relationship between the supply of and demand for goods. But imbalances are corrected either spontaneously or through preventive or corrective intervention by the monetary authorities.

The overall surplus is subject to two opposing forces. On the one hand, it grows through successive production increases. On the other, it decreases as a result of the double pressure for sharing arising from the market and the state. This double pressure is largely apparent in an increase in labour remuneration, either for the purpose of increasing their participation in the benefits of productivity gains or to be recovered through (directly or indirectly imposed) taxes or other fiscal measures, allowing the state to cover the social consumption of the labour force, its employment, be it necessary or spurious, and its acquisition of goods and services in the market.

If the rise in costs occasioned by increased remunerations exceeds the drop in costs resulting from increased productivity, the excess is carried over to prices. And if labour has sufficient power to make its retaliation effective, an inflationary spiral is set in motion. Under such conditions, if the supply which has been boosted by the increased costs is to be absorbed, it is essential that demand and income from which it arises increase correlatively.

If the monetary authorities oppose the necessary creation of money with the intention of preventing or checking the spiral, the growth of demand will be insufficient in comparison to final production. Thus, recession occurs in the economy and disequilibrium will persist until the monetary authorities change their minds and prices can rise in accordance with the raised costs. The rise in prices allows the surplus to increase, although only momentarily, since a further increase in remuneration again reduces it. Accumulation thereby decreases with consequent adverse effects on development in addition to the upheavals caused by the ensuing exacerbation of the distributive struggle. The same thing occurs if companies use the surplus for this purpose at the expense of their own demand, which will consequently be insufficient and will occasion a recession in the economy. It is to be noted, however, that these phenomena occur when, in the course of the democratisation process, labour unions and political power are continuously expanded, in both the market and the state spheres, and the latter's expenditure rises considerably as a result of its own dynamic.

In these conditions, the spiral comes to form an integral part of development of the periphery. And the conventional rules of the monetary game prove powerless to avoid or suppress it. These rules are especially valid when the ability to impose surplus sharing does not exist or is in its early stages. This occurs when the democratisation process is very weak or is obstructed or manipulated by the dominant groups. This explains how the economic disruption and social disintegration which occur during the unobstructed course of the democratisation process, in conjunction with the inflationary spiral, lead to the use of force in order to break up labour union and political power. It is then possible to restore the surplus and the dynamic of the system through a new boost given to the privileged consumer society.

The rules of the monetary game may then recover their efficacious ness, although this is not always the case. In fact, when inflatio originates outside the process, as is the case with a fiscal deficit, an attempt to bridle it by restricting the money supply required b circulating capital is counterproductive. In fact, the rise in prices cause by the deficit requires an increase in the creation of money in th productive process. If companies fail to obtain this, a recession sets i while prices continue to rise as an increasingly serious deficit persists o account of the recession. Formerly, a phenomenon of this nature did nc occur since the rules of the monetary game could be applied.

THE GREAT PARADOX OF THE SURPLUS

Important conclusions may be drawn from the preceding points, whic cover those elements that are perhaps of greatest importance in ou interpretation of capitalism on the periphery. We continue with summary of these conclusions.

By reason of the fact that only a part of the benefits of technologica progress is transferred to the labour force, the surplus acquired by th owners of the means of production grows at a higher rate than th overall product. Thus, the upper-income brackets, where most of th means of production are concentrated, may increase their capita accumulation and, in turn, their privileged consumption. The syster functions normally while accumulation grows continuously. For thi reason, it is essential that the surplus likewise increases. This essentia condition is fulfilled when the sharing of the surplus in the interplay c power relations, in both the market and the state spheres, occurs at th expense of successive productivity increases. The surplus will continu to grow although it be at a decreasing rate. But sharing cannot excee the limit beyond which the surplus begins to decrease.

However, upon reaching this limit, the surplus stands at its highes proportion in relation to the global product as well as to th accumulation and consumption of the upper-income brackets. So, wh should sharing not continue to improve when such a margin exists fo doing so, by reducing the surplus?

This is the weak point of the accumulation and distribution system. I was explained previously that if the double pressure of sharing exceed the increase in productivity, the ensuing increase in the cost of good leads companies to raise prices. Without a doubt, the global surplu could accommodate significantly more sharing at the expense of its size But there is nothing in the system which would allow this to take place. I might be imagined that companies would take a part of the surplus and pass it on to the labour force without raising costs. This would be a case of direct participation in the surplus. But the system does not function in this manner. Any rise in remuneration which exceeds the increase in productivity leads to a rise in costs, with the results mentioned above.

All the same, the full weight of the pressure to share does not make itself felt in the rise in remunerations. Above, we examined the case in which the state imposes taxes and other measures that fall on the labour force, in order to acquire a share in the surplus. This leads the latter to compensate by means of seeking increased remuneration. But the state can also directly tax the surplus or income of the upper social brackets who have no means of recouping their losses. These taxes are not carried over to costs but, should their extent exceed the productivity increase, the ensuing decrease in the surplus exercises an unfavourable effect on accumulation which, in turn, reduces the rate of growth, thereby accentuating the exclusive and conflictive tendencies of the system.

From whatever angle, this problem has no solution when the power to impose sharing is strengthened in an unhampered democratisation process. Either an inflationary spiral is set in motion when sharing results in an increase in the costs of production, which jeopardises the dynamic of the surplus quite apart from the upheavals caused by the spiral itself, or resources are taken directly from the surplus with adverse dynamic effects which will sooner or later have to be resolved with inflationary expedients.

For all the thought that has been given to this subject, the nature of the system makes it impossible to attack the two major defects of capitalism on the periphery: neither its exclusive nature, which could only be corrected through a more intense accumulation of capital at the expense of the privileged groups, nor its conflictive nature, which becomes increasingly pronounced in the interplay of power relations.

This question harbours a major paradox. When the global surplus reaches its maximum proportion of the global product, thereby providing the resources necessary to combat these effects, the system reacts by attempting to maintain and continue to boost the surplus. And the only way of doing so is to bring force to bear in order to suppress the power of the labour force to impose sharing. The use of force is not a solution. There is no alternative solution to the problem other than transforming the system.

III TOWARDS A THEORY OF TRANSFORMATION

CRISIS OF THE SYSTEM AND THE USE OF FORCE

In view of the nature of the system during the advanced stages of development on the periphery and of the democratisation process, it is impossible to avert the tendency towards this crisis. There is no definitive means of preventing this double sharing pressure, both in the market and the state spheres, from adversely affecting the dynamic role of the surplus, which inevitably brings on an inflationary spiral. Experience has shown that attempts to restore the dynamics of the system through the use of force are subject to a series of disturbances which usually involve the combination of theoretical inconsistencies and practical incongruencies.

However, if the system is skilfully managed, especially in a climate of favourable external conditions, high rates of accumulation and development can be achieved, accompanied by high levels of prosperity for the privileged social groups but at the expense of a sharp cut-back in income for a considerable proportion of the labour force. But this would not serve to correct the conflictive and exclusive nature of the system. And with the eventual resumption of the democratisation process the pressure exerted to achieve a share-out of the surplus would tend to carry the system into a new political cycle which would be aggravated by the deformation wrought in the productive structure in response to the elevation of the privileged consumer society.

THE TWO TRANSFORMATION OPTIONS

The system of accumulation and distribution of the benefits of technological progress is not subject to any regulatory principle from the point of view of the collective interest. Appropriation is arbitrary in the interplay of the laws of the market. Distribution is likewise arbitrary when political and labour union power counteract the laws of the market.

The state imposes a regulatory action in order to put the surplus to social use. There are only two basic forms of regulatory action: either the state takes over the ownership and management of the means of production from which the surplus originates or the state uses the surplus with collective rationality and imposes a social distribution of ownership as opposed to exercising exclusive control.

It might be mentioned in passing that the root of the major defects of the system is not the question of ownership itself but rather of private appropriation of the surplus and the harmful consequences of the concentration of the means of production. It is a question of two fundamentally different versions of socialism, in a political as well as an economic sense. Because, while the first version is not congruent with the primordial concept of democracy and its inherent human rights, the second version makes it possible to render the theory and practice of the concept mutually compatible and make these, in turn, concordant with development and distributive justice.

DIFFUSION OF CAPITAL AND AUTONOMOUS MANAGEMENT

The transformation of the system through the second of the above options necessarily requires an increase in the rate of capital accumulation at the expense of the consumption of the upper-income brackets and other favoured groups. Social use of the surplus allows this to be done in different ways.

In the companies in which the means of production are concentrated, greater accumulation could be achieved by transferring a large part of the surplus, in the form of new capital, to the labour force, not only that part of it working for the companies in question, but that in all companies.

In medium-sized companies, greater accumulation could be achieved by the owners themselves but as this amount rises higher up the capital ladder, a growing proportion would have to be transferred to the labour force in order to avoid concentration. In smaller companies, greater accumulation would be brought about solely by those who control the means of production. In large companies, this change in the social composition of capital would have to be accompanied by employee participation in management, until such time as autonomous management was fully established. Certain principles of this approach could also be employed in state companies, under given conditions justifying their use.

THE MARKET AND PLANNING

Within the new system, all companies, whatever their characteristics, could evolve freely in the market in accordance with certain basic conditions of an impersonal nature established by the regulatory action of the state with reference both to the social use of the surplus and other state responsibilities. The role of this regulatory action is to achieve objectives of which the market is incapable in itself but which will allow it to maximise economic efficiency and achieve a high level of social efficiency.

Democratic planning plays this role. Planning means collective rationality. This rationality requires that the surplus be directed towards accumulation and redistribution and also towards state investment and expenditure. Accumulation and redistribution are closely linked in that increasing productivity allows the labour force of the lower brackets to be absorbed as well as the labour spuriously employed by the system, thereby permitting redistribution to be improved. It is a case of dynamic redistribution of income accompanied by other direct forms of social improvement, in response to urgent needs. This redistribution of the surplus requires a major technical effort which cannot be successfully undertaken without a high level of functional autonomy: a technical as opposed to a technocratic effort, as it has to be subordinated to democratically established decisions taken by the political body.

The above requires constitutional changes in state mechanisms and new ground rules to ensure stability in the social use of the surplus as well as to allow for the flexibility necessary to respond to major changes in the situation.

SYNTHESIS OF SOCIALISM AND LIBERALISM AND THE STRUCTURE OF POWER

The transformation option put forward in these pages is a synthesis of socialism and liberalism: socialism in the sense that the state regulates accumulation and distribution; liberalism in that it basically postulates economic freedom closely bound up with political liberty in its original philosophic sense.

As was the case with the alternative socialist transformation option, this option requires major changes in the political power structure apart from those which occur through mutations in the social structure. As far as the latter changes are concerned, the power of the upper-income brackets is counterbalanced by that of the middle – and occasionally of the lower – income brackets. But in the context of the dynamics of the system currently in force, this power of enforcing sharing always comes up against the power of the existing system's dynamics. However, the crisis of the system opens up the way for transformation as the possibility of demolishing the power of the upper-income brackets is again presented. A crisis or, if this cannot be averted, the rise of a regime based on force.

These changes in the power structure could not extend beyond the limits of the periphery. Power relations between the periphery and the centres, under the hegemony of the latter and especially that of the major dynamic centre of capitalism, could not be changed on the basis of independent action taken by the periphery. The power of the centres is considerable and, furthermore, any sense of foresight is absent. This is amply apparent in the extensive damage being done to the biosphere. As is usual in the major crises in history, this may serve to convince the centres that their relations with the periphery must involve an ample degree of foresight and also of the restraint of power. I am inclined to believe that the restraint of its own power in the major dynamic centre of capitalism would have made it possible to avoid the current international monetary upheaval.

MYTHS AND TRANSFORMATION

The myth of the worldwide expansion of capitalism has evaporated as has the myth of development of the periphery in the image and likeness of the centres. The myths of the regulatory virtues of the laws of the market are also evaporating. Nobody could invoke them when confronted with the problems of the biosphere. But these myths persist with respect to the problems of the periphery and also to its relations with the centres.

Major transformations are thus called for. But it is necessary to know how and to what purpose such transformation is to be undertaken. The need for a theory of transformation is apparent. This paper was prompted by the urgent need for controversy and enlightenment and is offered as a contribution to the formulation of such a theory.

Comment on Dr Prebisch's Paper: 'The Latin-American Periphery in the Global System of Capitalism

Jagdish N. Bhagwati

Columbia University, USA

It is a privilege to be asked to be a Discussant of Raul Prebisch's Plenary Address. It is particularly appropriate that Prebisch is one of the distinguished plenary speakers at this congress in Mexico. For he is the Latin-American father of the field of development economics, sharing that pioneering role with Paul Rosenstein-Rodan, Ragnar Nurkse, Albert Hirschman and Arthur Lewis, to name the central figures that shaped the way developmental problems came into economic analysis after the war.

Prebisch's influential work on import-substitution strategy was unique in conception. As is well-known, he theorised about the tendency of the terms of trade to decline secularly against primary products. And he deduced from it the necessity for Latin America to industrialise via import substitution. In other areas of the developing world, the same developmental strategy was deduced from other analytical constructs. In India, for instance, few believed in the secular terms of trade deterioration thesis, but nonetheless 'elasticity pessimism' was combined with simple decision models such as the Feldman–Mahalanobis model to provide a theoretical rationale for an import-substitution strategy. And the same elasticity pessimism led to 'balanced growth' recommendations of both the Rosenstein-Rodan and Nurkse varieties, which equally implied an inward-looking import-substitution strategy. Interestingly, even the 'unbalanced growth' approach of Albert Hirschman implied import substitution as the preferred developmental strategy, since it led to what I call the 'slash (imports) and grow' version of industrialisation. Quite remarkably, therefore, the leading Suslovs of developmental economics at the creation of the field, Prebisch included, converged from different directions on to import-substitution strategy.

I recall Prebisch's role in this early embrace of import-substitution strategy to emphasise the originality of his thought and the intimate connection that it has had with his reflections on Latin-American experience. The same characteristics were evident in his early expression of the view that the import-substitution strategy should be tempered by regional trade liberalisation: a view that gathered momentum in the 1960s and preceded the major work on trade-and-developmental strategy (by Balassa for the World Bank; Little, Scitovsky and Scott for the OECD; and Bhagwati and Krueger for the NBER[1]) that has resulted in the current thesis that export-promoting strategy has many economic advantages over the import-substitution strategy.

The same originality and uniquely Latin-American conception are evident in Prebisch's address today. What he has said represents the culmination of ideas he has been developing since 1976 and he is tackling what are simply the most compelling questions in Latin America today: Is there an inherent connection between the growth of authoritarian regimes and the spread of global capitalism to the periphery, to use Prebisch's colourful terminology of the centre and the periphery? And, as corollary thereto: Can the invisible hand of Adam Smith work in the absence of the iron fist? Is it possible for economic liberalism to flourish if the political regime is not authoritarian? Interestingly, Professor Paul Samuelson's Plenary Address to this Congress raises very similar issues, from a very different perspective; that these questions are engaging the attention of some of the best minds in economics today is indisputable. Let me briefly summarise Prebisch's thoughts on this subject today, and then subject them to the careful scrutiny that they surely merit.

The core of Prebisch's argument consists of the following propositions, which I present in a stylised form, at the risk of some oversimplifications:

(1) The spread of capitalism to the periphery is essentially 'imitative' and involves 'the centres' propagation of their technology, patterns of consumption and other modes of cultural behaviour, institutions, ideas and technologies'.

(2) The interaction of this imitative capitalist process with the social structures in the periphery creates 'internal contradictions' in the developmental process in the periphery.

(3) Successful capitalism requires the creation and reinvestment of surplus.

---

[1] See Bela Balassa and associates, *The Structure of Protection in Developing Countries* (IBRD, Baltimore: The Johns Hopkins University Press, 1971); Ian Little, Tibor Scitovsky and Maurice Scott, *Industry and Trade in Some Developing Countries: A Comparative Study* (OECD, Oxford: Oxford University Press, 1970); Jagdish Bhagwati, *Foreign Trade Regimes and Economic Development: Anatomy and Consequences of Exchange Control Regimes* (NBER, Cambridge: Ballinger, 1978); and Anne Krueger, *Foreign Trade Regimes and Economic Development: Liberalization Attempts and Consequences* (NBER, Cambridge: Ballinger, 1978).

(4) However, the 'upper-income' groups 'imitate the centres' patterns of consumption', thereby causing a 'considerable wastage in capital accumulation potential'.

(5) At the same time, the 'middle groups' bring their 'union power' to bear on the system to increase their share of the pie and thus further cut into the investible surplus. This phenomenon works also through the state where these middle groups use their political power to 'obtain social services and increases in (presumably redistributive, rather than productive) employment'. The middle groups also tend to imitate the centres' patterns of consumption, though to 'a much lesser extent than the upper-income groups', thus accentuating the erosion of the surplus.

(6) The dynamic of the capitalist system in the periphery therefore involves a fundamental tension, with the surplus subject to pressure from the dual causes just described, whereas the 'companies react by raising prices in order to restore the dynamic of the surplus'. This tension results in an 'inflationary spiral of a social origin' which is accompanied also by inadequate accumulation and attendant failure to absorb 'the growing labour force which consequently vegetates in the lower brackets'.

(7) Faced with this crisis, the upper-income groups react by utilising military power as the tool with which to break the inflationary spiral and to restore the surplus at the expense of the middle and lower groups: 'Force is then brought to bear in order to break the labour union and political power held by underprivileged groups'. In short, capitalism in the periphery, given the imitative consumption of the upper and middle groups and the erosion of the surplus that follows from this, and also from the democratic system which permits the middle groups to obtain increased consumption through the state, leads almost inevitably to the rise of authoritarianism. This authoritarianism is then used to restore the surplus (except, presumably, for that part which is eroded by the upper-income groups themselves through their continued imitation of the centres' consumption patterns) so as to recreate the dynamic of the capitalist system; at the same time, 'to restore the regularity of development', the authoritarian state proceeds to establish economic liberalism: 'a laissez faire policy is established'.

Let me compliment Prebisch on the imaginative and stimulating sweep of his argument, while proceeding to differ from him on the detail of his thesis. My differences from him on the specific components of his argument should not distract from the considerable merit of his work; for, in economics as in other social sciences, it is far more important to raise the right questions than to answer the wrong questions correctly.

It appears to me that Prebisch's argument, while I sympathise with its general direction, is premised on a view of 'imitative development' which may be unable to support the structure he builds on it. Why should we conclude that the upper-income groups' pattern of consumption, because it is imitative, implies a reduction of the surplus? I believe that here Prebisch may be close to embracing the fallacy of misplaced concreteness: namely, that since upper-income groups consume luxury goods which were conceived in the centres and then diffused to the periphery, this must imply that the rate of saving will be less. If these particular types of goods were not consumed, however, it surely does not follow that others would not be, that the effect would be to increase savings, that is the surplus. This tendency to associate specific forms of consumption with the overall decision to save, or with the actual *ex-post* saving rate, has little theoretical or empirical support. Indeed, in my view, it has been an important source of inefficiency and failure of planning that some economists and policy-makers have tended to anthropomorphise goods into 'goods' and 'bads', equating the latter with certain undesirable outcomes. In my own country, for example, the Indian planners were advised to keep away from producing 'luxury' goods such as cars, on the rather ridiculous assumption (in retrospect) that these would add to consumption and thus reduce savings. The fact that these luxury goods could be exported and could buy the investment goods that could support higher savings, or that if these goods were not available then the consumers would buy other consumer goods, was not really understood. It is telling, therefore, that while Hindustan Motors in India, founded by the major industrialist group of Birlas in the same year that Toyota in Japan started manufacture of cars (both had started with producing cycles first), was left severely constrained in its production by controls from an ill-advised government and is still producing a ridiculously small amount of cars for the domestic market at high cost under protection, Toyota has become a major exporter to the world markets. I would urge caution therefore in accepting without careful scrutiny this rather easy assumption that production or consumption of luxury goods is somehow inimical to savings.

But Prebisch does not really need this extremely weak argument to sustain his major thesis that capitalist systems in the periphery are subject to serious pressures, especially when combined with political

pluralism. Pluralistic systems do tend to create precisely the pressures
for increased consumption that Prebisch identifies so well: trade union
pressures to increase wages; middle classes functioning through the
political system to reduce taxes, to increase benefits and thereby to
increase their real incomes at the expense of governmental savings; all
politically influential groups using public-sector employment to produce essentially redistributive jobs for their class members, either in the
civil service or in the military establishment or in public-sector
enterprises; and so on. The *macro* pressures therefore *are* rather difficult
to handle in a democratic set-up; and in developing countries, especially,
the 'politics of scarcity' seems to push the politicians in power in
pluralistic systems constantly close to the edge where they itch to impose
through force, or some form of negation of democracy, the macro-
discipline to sustain investment and therewith the economic growth that
is so critical to satisfying the aspirations for increased jobs and incomes.
Where the macro-discipline does not exist, economic liberalism also
tends to break down. For what Prebisch beautifully describes as the
'social disruption' following on the macro-pressures often leads the
government into a series of quantitative interventions to ration and to
share equitably, giving up on allocative efficiency. Where the macro-
discipline is restored by militaristic intervention, or by steps short of it as
in Mrs Gandhi's emergency phase in India, a concomitant result then
may well also be the restoration of economic liberalism.

I do not believe that economists, or political scientists for that matter,
can arrive at deterministic laws relating the iron fist to the invisible hand.
Much depends on the political and economic structures of the country
on the periphery. I am afraid that Prebisch weakens his case by
attempting a firm and unique linkage between the growth of authoritarianism and the spread of capitalism to the periphery. In fact, for Latin
America itself, others have attempted to trace the growth of authoritarianism to other types of economic factors: for example, a
Gerschenkron-type argumentation suggesting that the shift from easy
'first-phase' import substitution in consumer goods industries to the
more difficult 'second-phase' import substitution in heavy industries
legitimised the necessity of a more active role by the state in the
developmental process, and hence the takeover by the military or
otherwise-authoritarian forces. And, in India, the authoritarian phase
was extremely short-lived and was characterised by a remarkable return
to political democracy plus a firmer commitment to economic
liberalism.

In conclusion, let me compliment Raul Prebisch on raising so cogently, and in a most stimulating fashion, the important broad issues that confront economists as they contemplate the analysis of development. We economists have a tendency to retreat into narrowly technical issues where neat conclusions emerge because the big and relevant factors have been ruled out from our analysis. Prebisch's work helps to keep the larger picture in view and will surely serve to redirect our focus towards problems of central importance.

Comments on Dr Prebisch's Paper: 'The Latin-American Periphery in the Global System of Capitalism'

Bo Södersten

Sweden

Dr Prebisch has for a long time been a very influential economist indeed. When it comes to thinking about development issues his influence has been especially strong and persistent. His paper today is again a stimulating exercise, that will give us food for thought for a long time to come, and that we probably will not be able to digest fully in the course of one day.

I do not think that anyone would like to question the fact of Dr Prebisch's influence on policy matters. However when it comes to the theoretical structure of Dr Prebisch's argument economists in the western tradition have had some difficulties. It was often quite intricate. The assumptions of the analysis were more realistic than the ones often used in standard neo-classical analysis, as Dr Prebisch took the possibilities of collusion, both between firms in developed countries against consumer and labour, and between labour and industry in rich countries against labour and capital in poor countries, into account. In parts of the analysis the reasoning was easy to follow, as a simple supply-demand model was at the bottom of the argument. This was the case with the argument about worsening terms of trade for primary-producing countries, due to low income elasticities for their products. But there were other propositions, for instance about the effects of business cycles on the terms of trade, about the role of trade unions, and about the effects of market forms on international trade, that were more difficult to see through.

Today I will not go nit-picking, but try to take a somewhat broader view in my comments and assessment of Dr Prebisch's contribution. I think it is fair to say that in his writings Dr Prebisch has continually stressed two basic propositions. One is that resources at hand should be used fully. The other is that income-distribution aspects should always be taken into consideration. The first proposition is really one about economic rationality. It may sound commonsensical, not to say trite. But for developing countries the question of using existing resources fully is central. It has also come to the centre in industrialised countries, as growth rates have dropped and unemployment is steadily increasing and seems to be taking on a chronic character during the 1970s. So the problem of capacity utilisation is now a central issue, both in the centre and at the periphery, to use Prebisch's terminology. Income distribution issues may seem normative in nature. They certainly have aspects of a normative kind. But questions concerning income distribution also have their place in positive economics. We should not only be concerned with the effects of supply shocks or demand and parameter changes on aggregate incomes, price levels, total supplies and the like; we should always be prepared to ask the question 'cui bono?', for whom is a change bad or good, and be prepared to trace through the effects on factor prices and income distribution, both within and between countries. Developments in recent years, especially during the 1970s, have fully vindicated Dr Prebisch's main approach as questions of capacity utilisation and income distribution have again come to the forefront.

The debate around import-substitution has been raging for quite a few years. One of the important inspirations behind policies of import-substitution was an urge to use resources more fully, which implied allocative efficiency as well as resource mobilisation and the full use of available technology and equipment, instead of simply relying on established comparative advantages in primary products. In countries where such policies were applied indiscriminately they worked for a while, but tended to become self-defeating, as various types of distortions, bottlenecks and rigidities were introduced. In other countries they were more successful in preparing the ground for competitive industries. Timing is here essential. Setting up industries behind protection, while at the same time increasing productivity in agriculture, will pave the way for an export-push type of policy that can make a country competitive in international markets. The point here is that one has to work on the supply side continuously, in order to develop resources and use them efficiently. In order to achieve the latter, the exchange rate has to be watched carefully, so as to avoid the introduction of unnecessary distortions. I will be content with these comments on import-substitution as Dr Bhagwati has already treated this theme.

Market forms certainly can be important in determining the income distribution within a country. They may also have powerful implications for the international income distribution. Dr Prebisch was one of those who were to stress that, if monopolistic competition was prevalent among industrial countries, that could have harmful effects on the less developed countries, for instance by lowering their terms of trade. It is actually not quite clear whether monopolistic market conditions in the DCs have negative effects on the LDCs or not. In a dynamic setting monopolistic competition may foster growth, and this should spill over to the LDCs, both via reduced prices for their import products, and via an increased demand for their export products. Whether or not there has been a secular trend in the net barter terms of trade to the disadvantage of the primary-producing countries, is, as we know, a debatable question. I suppose one can, by leaving out oil, construct a negative case for the primary-producing countries, but even then, the deterioration would appear to be modest.[1]

By hindsight the earlier decades of the after-war era, the 1950s and 1960s, look quite like a golden age, at least from the point of view of the industrial countries, but also from the viewpoint of many developing countries. The 1970s turned out to be a much more problematic decade, with high rates of inflation and unemployment and increasing inequality, both within and between countries. The prospects for the 1980s also look quite bleak. As rates of capacity utilisation have been falling and income distribution becomes more skewed, a Prebisch type of approach would seem to gain increased relevance. Let me then make a few comments on recent events *à la mode de Prebisch*.

A dominating event in the international economy of the 1970s was the oil price hike of 1973–74. At the centre of the oil crisis was a redistribution of income. In 1973 the exports of the OPEC-countries had amounted to roughly US $30 billion. In 1974 they quadrupled to US $120 billion. Only small changes in quantities were involved. That meant that some US $90 billion were redistributed from the countries importing oil to the OPEC countries. The most important aspect of the oil price hike in 1974 is the income redistribution aspect and the effects on savings and investment that followed in its wake. Total savings increased drastically, as the OPEC countries spent less than 50 per cent of their total proceeds. In order to absorb the increased savings and keep equilibrium in the world economy, new investment outlets would have to be found. The only group of countries that could really swallow investments of this magnitude were the OECD countries. So on the international level the problem really boiled down to a *transfer problem* between the OPEC and the OECD countries. If that problem could have been solved in an orderly way, the growth of the world economy would have increased, because of an overall increase in saving and investment at the world level.

But, alas, no such development occurred. World leaders were not ready to see the new situation as it was, and act rationally. On the contrary, some rattlings of swords occurred, and resentment was felt at the so-called injustice implied in the new higher prices of oil. There was also a genuine uncertainty prevailing, as it undoubtedly was difficult to

[1] Cf. J. Spraos, 'The Statistical Debate on the Net Barter Terms of Trade between Primary Commodities and Manufactures', *Economic Journal*, 90 (March 1980).

say if the new prices were sustainable equilibrium prices. Many economists asserted at the time that they were not, and that the OPEC cartel would break down. There may have been some intellectual respectability behind that view. It also had the advantage of being a popular view. In the choice between the comfortable lie and the awkward truth, the latter is often the victim. In the absence of any genuine efforts at international co-operation every country had to fend for itself. The oil price hike meant a sharp price increase in critical intermediate goods, whose substitution elasticities were low. They created important effects in both goods and labour markets, and had strongly negative effects on trade balances in many importing countries.

At given incomes, we would expect the aggregate supply curve in the importing countries to shift to the left, creating an excess demand in the goods market. As less intermediate goods are produced, we would at the same time expect the demand for labour to fall. Thus we would have an excess demand in the goods market and an excess supply in the labour market. This would entail a stagflationary situation, where we at the same time had an inflationary pressure in the goods market and unemployment. This type of mechanism characterised, I think, most oil-importing countries in the middle of the 1970s. The picture then became further complicated by the presence of flexible exchange rates where many countries had depreciating exchange rates due to falling export demand, which further increased inflation.

This story can readily be interpreted in a Prebischian fashion. It is obvious that it had implications for income distribution, both at the national and international levels. It is true that real wages in many countries would have to fall, and so they did. But the application of restrictive monetary policies, operating on the demand side, often only made matters worse. An increase in supply factors, for instance, by means of tax credit for investments, subsidies to energy conservation, and lowering of payroll taxes, would instead have alleviated the situation.

This scenario also highlighted another of Prebisch's fundamental concepts, that of import-substitution. What were really needed in this situation – and should have been given first priority – were policies to reduce the use of oil. Countries ought to have tried to develop alternative sources of energy; to have relied on a straightforward policy of import-substitution. The only difference from traditional import-substitution policies was that they now had to be used primarily by industrial countries, to lower their demand for a critical import product. Unfortunately very few import-substitution measures were implemented. Some countries even tried to cushion the effects of the oil price hike, by not letting price increases work fully through into domestic markets. This was not a very wise policy from the point of view of curtailing demand and encouraging the development of alternative energy sources. A new complacency started to grow, as oil was coming forward in plentiful supplies from 1975 onward at the new price, which was even slightly falling in real terms. But eventually demand would outstrip supply. This happened in 1979. In part it can surely be said that the industrial countries brought the second oil price hike on to themselves by not taking import-substitution policies seriously enough.

If one looks with a somewhat broader perspective, the developments during the 1970s have had powerful impacts on the world economy. Growth rates have slowed down, especially in industrial countries, while capacity utilisation has fallen and unemployment has risen. New centres of economic power have come to the forefront, as witnessed by the oil-producing countries. An important factor has been the emergence of the so-called NICs, the new industrial countries, which have showed a remarkable export performance.

The concept of centre and periphery has thus changed considerably over the last decade. The industrial countries are no longer undisputed leaders in the world economy. They have grave economic problems on their hands, which it is doubtful if they can solve successfully; in many industrial countries unemployment rates will probably continue to be high, and many youngsters will confront a tight labour market that has little to offer them. Professor James Tobin has calculated that to bring the inflation rate in the United States down from about 10 to 2–3 per cent, using traditional monetary and fiscal policies, will entail a full decade of 10 per cent unemployment.[2] The oil countries will continue to play a central role, and the emerging industrial countries will continue their inroads into established export markets.

The prospects for the 1980s may seem bleak. Risks for an increased protectionism are quite great. For this reason alone, countries are probably wise to keep in mind policies toward self-reliance using import-substitution methods; as I have tried to show, such policies may be profitable, just because of rapidly changing opportunity costs due to as sharp price changes as those we have witnessed in the 1970s. But the gains to be had from increased international co-operation are also great. If countries could solve in an efficient way the transfer problem that is

[2] J. Tobin, 'Stabilisation Policy Ten Years After', *Brookings Papers on Economic Activity* (forthcoming).

inherent in the trade between OPEC and the rest of the world (and in particular the OECD-countries), that would probably be the single most important contribution toward an improving economic world order that could be made. More drastic measures of encouraging trade with, and development assistance to, the poorest nations are necessary, if these nations are not to be left out in the cold. Here the Brandt Commission has pointed to some bold measures. Whether an approach such as that proposed by the Brandt Commission is politically feasible remains, however, to be seen.

In the last part of his paper Dr Prebisch proposes what he calls a synthesis between socialism and liberalism. His ideas seem to be reminiscent of a system of workers' control or a system of a labour-managed economy. Under such a system the means of production are owned by the state or a larger social entity. The optimal rate of savings is determined by the state. But incentives are basically geared toward the performance of the individual labour-managed firm which has ample incentives both to increase productivity and to accumulate capital. It is easy to envisage that the introduction of such a system would encounter difficulties. But a movement along these lines may, as Dr Prebisch hints, be part of the future.

I will end my brief comments on Dr Prebisch's paper with these words. In years to come I am certain that economists and statesmen in various parts of the world will continue to read and be inspired by – and perhaps want to contradict – the writings of Raul Prebisch as he has presented them over the years and in his paper here today.

3 The World Economy at Century's End

Paul A. Samuelson

USA

I FUTUROLOGY

George Bernard Shaw declared, 'Those who can, do. Those who can'
teach'. Today's cynic says, 'Those who are able to predict, make the
econometric forecasts. Those who can't, become futurologists'. So, a
the beginning, let us make a deposition that no scientist can pinpoint th
distant future with any accuracy. What separates the sage from th
dilettante is the plausibility of the odds quoted, the degree of interest an
relevance in the tale told. History has shown us that the luck of clown
has often beaten that of sages. But for every number on the wheel there
some clown to give it backing; and so, once again, we must judge th
worth of a prophet by the *ex ante* plausibility of his model.

1980 is twenty years from the twenty-first century. To discern the roa
ahead whom should I learn from? Nostradamus is not my cup of tea
There is really nothing in Adam Smith, David Ricardo, or even Robe
Malthus that will serve my purpose. The world does not have
rendezvous with a classical steady state characterised by population ju
big enough to yield minimum subsistence wages.

Can the vision of Karl Marx be my guide? Since Marx was writin
more than a century ago, it would be no fair criticism of him if we foun
his paradigms obsolete. But, actually, the laws of motion of th
capitalistic system as recorded in the economic historians' annals for th
century after the 1867 publication of *Das Kapital* are not those sung b
Karl Marx; nor are the recorded patterns of real output and wage/prop
erty income shares deducible from the Marxian paradigms of surplu
value and organic composition of capital. Marx, the political scientis
merits a better report-card grade than Marx the political economist. A

58

least one-third of humanity lives under socialism; and nowhere, not even in Switzerland or Chicago, does anyone live under laissez faire nineteenth-century style.

Many are called as prophets. Henry Adams, Oswald Spengler, Leon Trotsky and Pitrim Sorokin, Arnold Toynbee, John Maynard Keynes, Friedrich Hayek, Joseph Schumpeter, Herman Kahn, the Club of Rome. Though many are called, few are chosen as seers by the score-keeping historian.

II KEYNES AND THE CONQUEST OF POVERTY

Not all prophets are equally bad. As Justice Oliver Wendell Holmes would put it, the cynicism of Joseph Schumpeter gives us a better run for our money than the mysticisms of Arnold Toynbee. Forty years after Friedrich Hayek wrote down his nightmare of the welfare state leading remorselessly to the totalitarian murder of freedom, Scandinavians enjoy freedom second to none that the world has ever seen; and, contrary to the logic of *The Road to Serfdom*, societies such as Chile and Singapore with maximal market freedoms live under dictatorships that suppress civil liberties.

For the purpose of today's discussion, I want to concentrate on the visions for the future of two great economists: John Maynard Keynes and Joseph Schumpeter. Each was born in 1883, the year that Karl Marx died. Each died not long after the Second World War.

Of the two, Keynes was the more optimistic. In 1930, before the Great Depression, Keynes wrote a remarkable essay called, 'Economic Possibilities for our Grandchildren'. He looked ahead for one hundred years – to the period I am focusing on today. He prophesised that by the early twenty-first century the stock of capital would have doubled, and doubled again, and redoubled still once more. As Keynes points out, there is nothing remarkable in this, only the grinding away over a long time of compound-interest growth at 2 per cent per annum. Reinforcing the accumulation of capital, Keynes predicted, would be technological innovation, the fruits of science, engineering and managerial rationalisation. With population under volitional control, this had to mean a four-to-eight fold increase in per capita living standards in progressive countries.

So, three decades before Galbraith, Keynes foretold the withering away of the problem of economic scarcity. Four decades before the sociobiology of Edward O. Wilson, Keynes warned that the human race had evolved in the grim Darwinian struggle for existence. He worried whether, once the machine freed us from the necessity to fight for our daily bread, our muscles would go flaccid and our boredom would drive us into a collective nervous breakdown. Anomie, neurosis, soft and hard drugs in the affluent suburbs – all these fit in nicely with the Keynesian horoscope.

In fact, Keynes correctly foretold the miracle progress that the modern mixed economy actually enjoyed in the third quarter of the twentieth century. I have checked his back-of-the-envelope econometrics against the recorded findings of Simon Kuznets and Colin Clark, and it is remarkable how lucky Keynes turned out to be in his extrapolations.

But it is only in fairy tales that one can write down the ending: 'And so they lived happily ever afterwards'. Just as Karl Marx ended up historic history with a classless society in which the state had withered away and resources somehow got themselves economically organised, so the paradigm of Keynes ends in a kind of Swedish utopia. In this utopia the successful interactions of the accelerator and the multiplier are brought about by the not-for-profit Bank of England and they serve to free the Bloomsbury élite to spend their days in artistic creation and their nights in the pleasures of friendship.

III SCHUMPETER'S SCHIZOPHRENIC SCHEMATA

Perhaps in 1965, under the spell of John F. Kennedy's Camelot, one could have confidence in the verisimilitude of the Keynesian trajectory of economic development. In 1980, with the disappointing memories of the 1970s fresh in mind, the darker horoscope of Joseph Schumpeter gains in relevance. Schumpeter wrote *Capitalism, Socialism and Democracy* a decade after Keynes presented his vision of the future. The Great Depression showed Schumpeter how prone the political systems of Europe and North America were to depart from the conventional patterns and practices of constitutional democracy. Since Joseph Schumpeter had earlier lived through the decay of the feudal society in Austria-Hungary, and had observed with some distaste its replacement by fragile bourgeois establishments, he was better prepared than most of us for the happenings of the Hitlerian age.

You must also remember that Schumpeter was isolated in Cambridge Massachusetts during the Second World War. Students were few. Most of his colleagues had been called into the war effort. Living in

Cambridge and commuting to Cornwall, Connecticut, Schumpeter was not in very close touch with how the war was actually proceeding. Thus, I can testify from personal memory, that as late as 1943 or 1944 Schumpeter still expected that Hitler would end up victorious. When the actual reality came to be realised, he was saddened by the expectation that the Soviet Union would be the true victor of the war. In Schumpeter's view, we had been engaged with the wrong ally in fighting the wrong enemy. Since Joseph Schumpeter was not a very diplomatic person and since he took pleasure in shocking people, you can be sure that his views were not very popular in those wartime days.

I think it would be wrong, however, to believe that Schumpeter's view of the future was formulated after 1940. If we read him with care, we can see that already in the 1920s Schumpeter had arrived at the following schemata of history.

SCHUMPETER'S AXIOM 1: THE ECONOMIC SYSTEM ITSELF IS ESSENTIALLY STABLE

Walrasian general equilibrium always has a solution and such a solution would be capable of realising itself if the political and sociological system would permit economic laws to operate.

To be sure, Schumpeter had a dynamic theory of innovation and development. Entrepreneurial innovation, which Schumpeter associated with a particular sociological type, would be enabled by the money-creating banking system to upset and disturb the Walrasian equilibrium. Booms and high temporary profits would result from bursts of innovation. But then the mills of imitative competition would grind fine and erode away the transient profits. In all likelihood the return to Walrasian equilibrium would be accompanied by an overshot. But, in time, a laissez-faire capitalistic system would find its way back to a new Walrasian equilibrium with a higher standard of living, shared by workers and owners of natural resources.

I gloss over as not important for the present purpose the hoopla that Schumpeter liked to make about the different cyclical rhythms of capitalism. He took more seriously than a grown man should, the taxonomy of Kondratieff long waves, Juglar major business cycles averaging about eight years in duration, and the forty-month Kitchin–Crum shorter business cycles. His two-volume 1938 *Business Cycles* book goes into all this, but it never really commanded much attention in those first heady days of the Keynesian Revolution. And as Schumpeter himself fully recognised, it would not materially affect the validity of his

underlying vision if the reader rejected Schumpeter's belief in super
imposed business cycles. I may add that a disbelief in Schumpeter's zero
interest steady state need also have no material effect upon ou
acceptance or rejection of Schumpeter's vision of the innovationa
development process of creative destruction.

Before proceeding to Schumpeter's Axiom 2 from his Axiom 1 abou
the stability of the economic system in purely economic terms, I ought to
point out that this part of Schumpeter pretty much agrees with Keynes's
1930 horoscope. In writing up his 1942 book, Schumpeter may have
forgotten Keynes's 1930 arithmetic. But on his own he constructs a
similar compound-interest accumulation of capital that is helped in
stimulating productivity by an ongoing process of technological change
With a wave of his hand Schumpeter dismisses as preposterous the post-
1936 Keynesians' worry over the possibility of saving being in excess o
investment. Keynes in 1930 can be forgiven for not being concerned with
the dilemma of an economy that stagnates below its full-employmen
potential because of a mismatch between saving propensities and
motivated investment opportunities. Schumpeter can claim no similar
defence when he airily dismisses the stagnationist apprehensions of post-
Keynesian writers. Here Homer nods badly. Instead of invoking
theoretical arguments of the Pigou-effect type, or marshalling anti-
Hansen empirical trends in George Terborgh's manner, Schumpeter
merely asserts that most saving activity is itself motivated by investment
opportunity. So, depression psychology aside, Schumpeter claims that
consumption will spontaneously rise to fill the gap whenever investment
fails to be buoyant. For once, the ebullient Schumpeter shows his age.

There is one minor difference between the optimisms of Keynes and
Schumpeter. Keynes in 1930 is really talking about the future successes
not of capitalism but of what we have since come to call *the Mixed
Economy*. Schumpeter, by contrast, is dealing with the polar case of
unfettered capitalism. This archetypical mode is set up by Schumpeter
not as a projection of what is likely to prevail in the future, but precisely
as a contrafactual stalking horse to help make his point concerning the
political demise of capitalism. This leads me to Schumpeter's Axiom 2,
with its Hegelian negation of his Axiom 1.

SCHUMPETER'S AXIOM 2

Although the capitalistic system is *economically* stable, capitalism is
essentially *politically unstable*.

The very successes of market capitalism in delivering the goods of material progress, Schumpeter proclaimed, would lead to capitalism's undoing. That rationality of capitalism which makes for productivity will serve to corrode the irrational sentiments of social cohesiveness. The spoiled children of affluence will reject their parents and heritage. Their self-hate will lead to boredom and anomie. As I mentioned in my 1970 Nobel Lecture, Schumpeter, like Keynes, was an early sociobiologist. He believed that the economic problem of scarcity had selectively evolved the fitter modes of rational thinking. The need to be *homo economicus* was the Darwinian struggle that created *homo sapiens*.

As *Capitalism, Socialism and Democracy* approaches its fortieth birthday, what stands up best in its analysis is this striking thesis of Schumpeter that capitalism's very success will be its undoing. Joseph Schumpeter, looking down from Valhalla on the Iranian revolution against the Shah, must be crowing, 'I told you so!' In his view the same fate would have been meted out to Peter the Great were it not that the feudal elements of superstition and religion conspired to protect Peter from the Shah's destiny.

Schumpeter, like Thorstein Veblen, does not really document conclusively the interesting dogmas that he promulgates. Like Oliver Twist, we readers ask for 'More'.

Back in 1969, that Vietnam War era of New Left student revolts on American campuses, I wrote a column for *Newsweek* entitled 'Memories'. It dealt with the great evening in my life back at Harvard forty years ago when giants walked the earth in the Harvard Yard. Because of its relevance to the outlook for 1999, permit me to quote my *Newsweek* words.

Joseph Schumpeter, Harvard's brilliant economist and social prophet, was to debate Paul Sweezy on 'The Future of Capitalism'. Wassily Leontief was in the chair as moderator, and the Littauer Auditorium could not accommodate the packed house.

Let me set the stage. Schumpeter was a scion of the aristocracy of Franz Josef's Austria. It was Schumpeter who had confessed to three wishes in life: to be the greatest lover in Vienna, the best horseman in Europe, and the greatest economist in the world. 'But, unfortunately,' as he used to say modestly, 'the seat I inherited was never of the topmost caliber.'

Half mountebank, half sage, Schumpeter had been the *enfant terrible* of the Austrian school of economists. Steward to an Egyptian princess, owner of a stable of race horses, onetime Finance Minister of Austria, Schumpeter could look at the prospects for bourgeois society

with the objectivity of one whose feudal world had come to an end i
1914. His message and vision can be read in his classical work of a
quarter century ago, *Capitalism, Socialism, and Democracy.*

WHOM THE GODS ENVY

Opposed to the foxy Merlin was young Sir Galahad. Son of a
executive of J. P. Morgan's bank, Paul Sweezy was the best tha
Exeter and Harvard can produce. Tiring of the 'gentlemen's C' and o
the good life at Locke-Ober's with Lucius Beebe, Sweezy had earl
established himself as among the most promising of the economists o
his generation. But tiring of the conventional wisdom of his age, an
spurred on by the events of the Great Depression, Sweezy became on
of America's few Marxists. (As he used to say, you could count th
noses of American academic economists who were Marxists on th
thumbs of your two hands: the late Paul Baran of Stanford; and, in a
occasional summer school of unwonted tolerance, Paul Sweezy.)
Unfairly, the gods had given Paul Sweezy, along with a brilliant mind
a beautiful face and wit. With what William Buckley would de
sperately wish to see in his mirror, Sweezy faced the world. If lightnin
had struck him that night, people would truly have said that he ha
incurred the envy of the gods.
So much for the cast. I would have to be William Hazlitt to recall fo
you the interchange of wit, the neat parrying and thrust, and all mad
the more pleasurable by the obvious affection that the two men ha
for each other despite the polar opposition of their views.

MEETING OF OPPOSITES

Great debaters deserve great moderators, and that night Leontief wa
in fine form. At the end he fairly summarized the viewpoint
expressed.
'The patient is capitalism. What is to be his fate? Our speakers are i
fact agreed that the patient is inevitably dying. But the bases of thei
diagnoses could not be more different.
'On the one hand there is Sweezy, who utilizes the analysis of Mar
and of Lenin to deduce that the patient is dying of a malignant cancer
Absolutely no operation can help. The end is foreordained.
'On the other hand, there is Schumpeter. He, too, and rathe
cheerfully, admits that the patient is dying. (His sweetheart alread
died in 1914 and his bank of tears had long since run dry.) But t

Schumpeter, the patient is dying of a psychosomatic ailment. Not cancer but neurosis is the patient's complaint. Filled with self-hate, he has lost the will to live.

'In this view capitalism is an unlovable system, and what is unlovable will not be loved. Paul Sweezy himself is a talisman and omen of that alienation which will seal the system's doom.'

All this I had long forgotten. And a few years ago when I reread Schumpeter's book, I graded him down for his gloomy views on the progress that would be made by the mixed economy – capitalism in an oxygen tent, as Schumpeter put it. His failure to predict the miraculous progress of the postwar years earned Schumpeter a C in my eyes. However, 1969 university happenings reveal an alienation of privileged youth entitling Schumpeter to a report-card recount.

IV THE MIRACULOUS MID-CENTURY SPRINT

How are we to judge the respective merits of the views about the future in Keynes and Schumpeter? What would be most useful about my evaluation of these great economists resides in the fact that describing their hits and misses is an instructive way of formulating my own hunches about the years still ahead.

First, Keynes and Schumpeter did a pretty good job in estimating what modern economists call 'the trend of potential GNP' for the advanced nations of the world. This is not a task of superhuman complexity. Lay persons, and some crochety professionals, do manage to make gross errors in this regard. Mad dreamers see the end of the world at hand each weekend. Science fiction writers foretell incredible improvements in the standard of living just around the corner, and they find a ready audience among those disaffected with the here-and-now. But the sober analysis of statistical trends by a Simon Kuznets or Arthur Okun tells a less exciting but more credible tale. The greatest economists of my lifetime have been extraordinarily wise in guessing by rule of thumb what the more elaborate models of the cliometricians will derive after tedious calculation.

On the whole I judge that Schumpeter substantially underestimated the actual performance of the world economy in the third quarter of the twentieth century. His point was that 'fettered capitalism – capitalism in an oxygen tent' – could viably survive. But I do not see that he had the imagination or luck to perceive in advance the actual economic miracle enjoyed by Germany and Japan, Sweden and Switzerland, Western Europe generally and in particular the original Common Market countries.

This magnificent performance, if Schumpeter had been apprised of it, by the logic of his thought he would have had to regard as taking place *despite* the encroachment of the mixed economy on the prerogatives of market capitalism. I, by the advantage of hindsight, am forced to the quite opposing conclusion that the miracle decades of the 1950s and 1960s were actually *enhanced* by those encroachments of the mixed economy on laissez faire capitalism. Japan Inc. has neither the Walrasian structure of perfect competition nor the oligopolistic structure of Schumpeter's dynamic monopoly capitalism. The bureaucracy of the Bank of Japan and MITI played a vital role in the miracle.

All around the world, the post-Keynesian environment provided macroeconomic stimulus to employment and gave effective protection against deflation and persisting slump. After the successful Marshall Plan and MacArthur occupation of Japan, the ultimate fragilities of the Bretton Woods mechanism for a long time escaped recognition. In a fool's paradise, dollar undervaluation turned into dollar overvaluation, a disequilibrium that was papered over for the decade of the 1960s by uneasy acceptance of a flood of dollar IOUs.

I have often pondered over this basic question: Why did not Western Europe catch up with the United States after the First World War in the way that came to pass after the Second World War? I cannot fault Schumpeter for failing to prophesy this remarkable overtaking of America. But that failure does reveal him to be only human.

Sweden is an example I often use to calibrate Schumpeter's insights and outsights. Sweden may yet confirm Schumpeter's cynical pessimism, but if so Schumpeter's pessimism was certainly enunciated twenty-five years too early. From 1945 to 1970 neutral Sweden pulled off a veritable hat trick. Eschewing Schumpeter's old-fashioned socialism in the form of a governmental ownership of the means of production, Sweden achieved much egalitarianism by means of expanded tax-financed welfare payments. What is remarkable is the fact that she was able *to redivide the social pie without reducing its size or slowing down its rate of growth.* Fair shares coexisted with 8 per cent annual improvements in manufacturing productivity – something that Australians and New Zealanders only dream about but which rarely gets confirmed in the history books of any nation.

Alas, poor Hayek! His 1945 readers were quite unprepared for the statistical triumphs recorded a score of years later in the annals of the

OECD. Latter-day Marxists had to counter the demonstrated augmentations of proletarian real wage increases by the complaint 'What is material prosperity to an *alienated* worker?' Similarly, Doctors Hayek and Friedman on the right have had to take a leaf from the book of Ludwig von Mises and pooh-pooh as meaningless the index numbers of soaring real output calculated for economies like those in Western Europe which substantially second-guess the market place. And when that fails to serve as a sufficient discount, it is still open to them to complain, 'What is material prosperity to individuals who have lost their libertarian freedoms?'

V INEVITABILITY OF SOCIALISM?

To live is to change one's mind. Not uncommonly a sage will come to repudiate his own earlier classic. I could document from my own personal contacts with Joseph Schumpeter that he no longer believed in the 1940s what he taught me on my first 1935 afternoon in the Harvard Graduate School – namely that no large company like Du Pont or General Motors could continue to stay on top under the onslaught of new innovators. In his later writings Schumpeter was converted to the view that the modern large corporation has in a sense acquired the secret of perpetual youth and innovational rejuvenation.

But we happen to know that, up to the evening before he died, Schumpeter continued to believe that capitalism was on course to its rendezvous with socialism. Schumpeter's death was that which is a gift of the Gods. He died at his battle station, scholar's quill in hand, at the peak of his powers. He had all but finished the penultimate paragraph of his American Economic Association speech entitled 'The March to Socialism'. For once Schumpeter was trapped into the conventional wisdom. And it will help us peer with the rest of this decade's future if we engage in unsparing analysis of where Schumpeter may have gone wrong in his extrapolations.

Socialism may once have had a simple definition where the state owned the means of production – the land and mines, the factories and tools, inventories of raw materials and finished goods – that was socialism. By contrast under capitalism land, labour and capital goods were all privately owned and got allocated through the push-shove equilibrium of market competitions.

All this would have been understood by early socialist writers, by such Fabians as the Webbs and Shaw, and by the followers of Marx. They, and their capitalist critics, would have agreed that the October Revolution of Lenin converted Tsarist capitalism into socialism. And they would have agreed that an evolutionary acquisition by the British Government of ownership of the coal mines, railroads, banks and steel mills would have represented a march along the road from capitalism to socialism.

If you interpret Schumpeter's confident prediction that capitalism was on its way to socialism to mean that he expected the third quarter of the twentieth century to witness a burgeoning of governmental takeovers of the means of production, then we would have to award Schumpeter a failing grade on his forecast.

I believe Schumpeter realised this point. But he never really seemed to have clarified his thinking on the matter. When you broaden your definition of socialism so that you cannot be caught out in technical error, you may make the concept so fuzzy as to rob it of much of its usefulness.

Here is a personal anecdote to illuminate Schumpeter's ambiguities. Once at a cocktail party he said to me: 'I'd expect a socialist like you to believe that'. I was quite taken aback, being genuinely surprised, and asked, 'Do you really take me to be a socialist, Joe?' I pressed the point beyond that of perfunctory politeness to clear up my understanding of what Schumpeter's general views were. 'After all', I pointed out, 'I was brought up by the Chicago School under Frank Knight and Henry Simons. I first resisted the Keynesian revolution in macroeconomics. Do you regard anyone who believes in fiscal policy stabilisation and in New Deal welfare programmes as a socialist? By what single criterion would you, after knowing me these many years, define me to be a socialist?'

Schumpeter squirmed a bit. After all he was a polite man, and diplomatic behaviour does not compel unsparing truth. Finally, Schumpeter explained, 'My dear Paul, I was merely making reference to what you will not deny, that you lack respect for the pietistic verities of capitalism'.

There I must admit he had me. I fear I lack respect for most things; it is an imperfection in my nature. But leaving personalities, notice how broadening the definition of socialist to cover those who are cynical or even objective about capitalism – notice how this trivialises the proposition that, in the last half of the twentieth century, socialism will come to prevail.

For one thing it reduces to a redundant tautology Schumpeter's proposition that ideological disaffection with capitalism will create socialism. Disaffection cannot be said to create disaffection: disaffection *is* disaffection just as a rose is a rose and two and two are four, propositions not capable of being empirically refuted or meaningfully corroborated.

Somewhere Schumpeter proposes a more useful broadening of the word 'socialism' beyond its original connotation of state ownership of the means of production. He speaks of 'an extension of the public sector at the expense of the private sector' as constituting an extension of socialism. But in using this terminology Schumpeter comes back to being very close to Keynes and the New Deal liberals in the American sense of the word liberal. In the Schumpeter—Sweezy debate I referred to, it sounded ominous when Schumpeter predicted that the patient was dying even if only of a psychosomatic ailment. Death is, after all, no joke. But his listeners would have been less enthralled by his diagnosis if he had patiently explained to them that all he meant to say was that the patient was turning over a new leaf, entering upon a new life of jogging and vitamins and noble thinking along mixed economy lines.

I must repeat that Schumpeter's thought was confused. He really did not expect the mixed economy, whose evolution he correctly perceived, to be a well-functioning and stable way of running the railroad of modern social living. The fact that Schumpeter was, on the whole, wrong in this regard for the third quarter of the century should not blind us to the possibility that some of the malfunctionings he feared may be looming up more closely ahead in the last quarter of this century.

VI LATIN AMERICA AS PARADIGM

The human mind thinks in terms of overdramatic case-studies. I suggest that to understand the future there may be a more useful paradigm than that suggested by Scandinavia, the Netherlands, or a typical mixed economy of Western Europe or North America. I am not proposing that we concentrate on the Yugoslavian experiment or on the pattern of an Eastern European economy such as Hungary or Poland. Instead I have in mind the Latin American example.

Suppose someone in 1945 had asked: 'What part of the world do you expect to experience the most dramatic take-off in the next three decades?' Probably I would have given an answer something like the following: 'Argentina is the wave of the future. It has a temperate climate. Its density of population provides a favourable natural resource endowment per employee. By historical accident its present population is the fairly homogeneous progeny of Western European nations. And

Argentina is in 1945 at that intermediate stage of development from which rapid growth is most easily expected.'

How wrong I would have been. Nor would my prophecy have been much better if I had substituted Chile for Argentina. In point of fact the southernmost countries of Latin America have fallen most markedly below their post-war potentials for development. The reasons do not seem to be narrowly economic. We cannot explain what has happened by appeal to Malthus's law of diminishing returns. There has been no exogenous shift in world demands peculiarly unfavourable to that region of the world. Their sickness, Schumpeter would claim, is political and sociological rather than economic. It has to do with the breakdown of social consensus. It has to do with the workings out of the logic of populist democracy. A conservative like Schumpeter or Pareto or Sorel would agree in their diagnoses with the class-struggle analyses of Marxian writers. But with this difference. The Marxians would welcome battling between classes that gums up the working of capitalism. This is part of the temporary labour pains necessary if the benevolent permanent condition of communism is to get born. For Pareto and Schumpeter, by contrast, the death throes of the achieving market economy have the inevitability of a Greek tragedy, but are nevertheless in themselves pointless and regrettable.

Not being an expert on Latin America, I cannot pretend to give a definitive interpretation of its political malaise. It is superficial to blame the lack of progress on the dictator Juan Péron. Years after Péron had left Argentina, and before his return, chronic inflation and stagnating growth characterised that part of the world. It is ironical that Uruguay was once called the Switzerland of Latin America. (It is ironical in a different sort of way that Lebanon was once called the Switzerland of the Near East.)

VII THE WAY WE LIVE NOW

Oslo, Washington and New Delhi are a long way from Buenos Aires and Santiago. But is it far-fetched, as we try to peer into the decades just ahead and do so against the backdrop of the 1970's era of worldwide stagflation, to fear that many of our mixed economies will begin to suffer from their own version of the Argentinian sickness?

My implicit prediction is not that the recent inflation rates of 5 to 20 per cent will be revving up in the decade ahead to the South American rates of 30 to 200 per cent per annum. I do not regard that as particularly kely and it is not an essential part of my thesis that it should occur.

My point is a deeper one. We have eaten of the fruit of the Tree of Knowledge. Whether for Schumpeter's reason that capitalist success must breed alienation from it or for other reasons that I will advance, democratic societies do not adhere to self-denying practices and let the Walrasian game of pure economics play itself out. *The same self-interest that provided the gasoline to make the classical game of markets operate must be expected in today's political sphere to motivate interferences with the laissez faire scenario.*

This could be dignified as a theorem of von Neumann's theory of games.

Social equilibrium à la Queen Victoria or Calvin Coolidge is unstable. If all groups but one adhere to its modes of behaviour, then it definitely pays the remaining persons to form a collusion and use the state to depart from the laissez faire beloved by Ludwig von Mises or Fredric Bastiat.

It will not do to object to my implication with the riposte: 'But if all collusions and cliques try to second-guess the market, they may well *all* end up worse off than where Smith's Invisible (and unthinking) Hand would have taken them'. For it is also a theorem in the theory of non-zero-sum games that the Golden Rule state, which would make everybody happiest if all uniformly adhered to it, may itself be unstable. If some adhere to the behaviour it calls for, it pays others to depart from it in their own interest. Religion and superstition are invoked to propagandise for the Golden Rule precisely to alleviate this incipient instability.

Do not interpret me as saying that the mixed economy is intrinsically bad. It is not my belief that *any* interferences with laissez faire are on balance harmful. The neo-classical economists of goodwill had a noble and feasible vision. They advocated redistributive taxation and transfers to reduce the stark inequalities of laissez faire. Marshall, Wicksell and Pigou are instances in point. Economists also advocated macroeconomic stabilisation, whether of the Irving Fisher 1920 variety, the Keynes–Ohlin 1937 variety, or the Tobin–Friedman 1980 variety. And do-gooders like me envisage a role in the mixed economy for democratic policies designed to influence the fraction of high-employment GNP going to capital formation, and envision a measure of democratic planning to deal with externalities and probabalistic problems of the future.

All this is a noble vision, most of you will allow. But what guarantee is there that the forces of democracy will converge to those interferences with the market economy that are nicely optimal, forsaking all other temptations that involve deadweight loss and distortion?

Our reason does raise doubts. Experience, alas, does not quell these doubts. Examine the history of half a hundred former colonies that have achieved national independence in our time. For how many of them has the date of emancipation coincided with a Rostovian takeoff in the economic sphere? You know how sad the brute facts are in this domain. Even after we allow for a shake-down period of decline, the mismatch between performance and aspiration embalmed in formal five-year plans is painfully evident.

VIII STAGFLATION AS AN INHERENT FEATURE OF THE MIXED ECONOMY

My concern is not that of an élitist looking down with pity on the immaturities of developing countries. The bell I fear to be hearing tolls for the most affluent countries of North America and Western Europe – and also for Japan and Australia.

At this very moment the United States is in a genuine recession, and much of the world is in a growth recession. Well, what is so unusual about that? The history of capitalism was a history of boom and bust. There is the difference that *this recession is one deliberately contrived by governments*. If you had attended in this last year conferences of international economic authorities, you would have found that most of the central bankers and treasury officials present, to say nothing of a thinner majority of the academics in attendance, hoped for a recessionary slowdown. The reason is plain. They viewed the 'flation' part of the modern disease of stagflation as a greater evil than the 'stag' part. Neither their experience nor their reason tempted them to advocate mandatory price and wage controls as a better antidote than a contrived slowdown. A secondary factor reinforcing their advocacy was their hope that OPEC prices might be better contained if a deceleration of world activity lowered the demand for energy.

It is my thesis that stagflation is an intrinsic characteristic of the mixed economy. Back in 1973, I prepared a memorandum on *Worldwide Stagflation* for the West German Council of Economic Advisors. In it I gave a pessimistic diagnosis of the modern disease of stagflation. I hope my thesis is wrong, because it is so fundamental and traces the roots o agflation into the basic nature of the modern welfare state. In ummary, I attribute the mixed economy's stagflation to the fact that urs is now a humane society in which the presence of unemployment nd industrial slack is not permitted to have the downward repercussion n prices and wages that was characteristic of the cruel and ruthless apitalism of the history books.

I would think it a mistake to regard West Germany, Switzerland and apan as immune to the scourge of stagflation. It is true that elderly ankers all over the world envy these three countries for their relative egree of success in avoiding accelerating two-digit price inflation. witzerland has even for brief periods enjoyed stable prices. West ermany averaged an inflation rate in the late 1970s of below 4 per cent. apan's price index could not match these stellar performances but until cently was able to do better than most OECD countries.

But do not forget that this success on the price level front was urchased by all three countries at a fairly heavy cost in terms of vigour f output growth. The production index in Switzerland has barely covered to the pre-1973 level. For the decade of the 1970s real GNP owth in West Germany was slightly worse than that of the United ates, and in the last half of the decade was definitely worse. If witzerland and West Germany had not been able to sweep some of eir unemployment under the rug by putting its burden on guest-orkers, the crusade against inflation would have lost some of its dherents. Although it is true that Japan continues to display more rapid al growth than the other principal OECD countries, when I calculate ow much Japan has fallen below its extrapolated trend profile, I timate that the cost has been fairly steep for her to fight stagflation.

In concluding I must record the guess that world growth in the last uarter of the century must be estimated to be lower than that in the ird quarter. My colleague Charles P. Kindleberger is a coiner of xpressive titles. Kindleberger speaks of the 'menopausal economy'. his is not Wagnerian *Götterdämmerung*. Progress ebbs not with a bang ut with a whimper.

Such biological analogues may offer an expressive tag, but they rovide no true explanation. Opium puts you to sleep because of its ormative property. We age because of our aging. Modern economics an hope to do better than that by way of analysis.

Undoubtedly one reason for slower growth ahead is the fivefold ncrease in the real OPEC price of energy. This is usually called a cartel rice, but to me what requires explanation is not so much why the price now high as why the oil price was so very low in the years preceeding

1973.[1] Today's OPEC price may be more what economists ought to ca
competitive price than monopoly price. The major competitive cost
not the few dollars needed to suck oil out of the ground. The bas
marginal cost is that of future alternative use. If all oil were auctioned o
the way all wheat is, I would guess its price would vary from $20 to $80
barrel from month to month. A Three Mile Island incident that clouc
the future of nuclear energy everywhere except in the Soviet Union an
China, would rationally raise the equilibrium price of oil by several ter
of dollars. The ability and willingness of Saudi Arabia to provide th
umbrella of price stability is the one feature of OPEC that does smack c
monopolistic cartel rather than competition. To sum up, beside ol
other natural resources will presumably set limits on average glob.
growth now that so many countries have achieved the stage c
industrialisation that exhausts irreplaceable resources at a rapid rate

As a second factor making for deceleration in future growth rate
there is the let-up in effort and discipline that comes from affluence itsel
It is rational, not irrational, for Swedes and Americans to take longe
vacations, slow down the work pace on the job, talk back to th
foreman, and neglect the fine arts of spelling and algebra. South Korea
workers are hungrier than Belgian workers and some of their tecl
nological disadvantage can be offset by this factor of personal eagernes
As Germans and Japanese prosper, they too will in all likelihood acquir
the stigmata of affluence.

There is a third, less certain, reason for slower productivity chang
ahead. Schumpeter's process of innovation and technical chang
reached its zenith during the Second World War and the catch-up perio
thereafter. History is always a race between the law of diminishin
returns and the discovery of scientists. The rate of advance in pur
science and applied engineering is far from a stationary time-series. It
quite unpredictable in its oscillations, and these oscillations are not at a
like a white-noise process. The temporary period of Schumpeteria
monopoly power to extort the rents of innovation becomes a short
period in this age of rapid communication and public regulation. All i
all, we cannot count with any confidence on a renewed burst c
productivity emanating from scientists, engineers and managers.

[1] I think those prices were below true competitive price. My hypothesis t
explain this hinges on the fact that the dozen giant oil companies could not coun
on their property rights to drill for oil at the optimal rate. So, ignoring tru
(future) opportunity cost, they rushed to produce oil at more than warrantab
competitive rate in the pre-OPEC days.

IX THE DEVIL'S FIX THAT DOES NOT FIX

Clever members of my audience will have discerned one possible solution to the dilemmas of the mixed economy that I have dwelled upon. Vilfredo Pareto was a clever man. And so was Georges Sorel. Reading between Schumpeter's lines, I believe we can see that the same solution as theirs was tacitly in his mind even though it was only on a few private occasions that Joseph Schumpeter drew as advocate the obvious moral from his own insight.

What I am alluding to is of course the fascist solution. If the efficient market is politically unstable, then fascist sympathisers conclude: '*Get rid of democracy and impose upon society the market regime.* Never mind that trade unions must be emasculated and pesky intellectuals put into jail or exile.'

The 1980 Eleventh Edition of my *Economics* has a new section devoted to the distasteful subject of capitalist fascism. So to speak, if Chile and the Chicago boys had not existed, we should have had to invent them as a paradigm. It is relevant to quote some of my words – the more so because conservatives who dislike how democracy works out are unwilling to follow their logic to the fascist conclusion these days and use constitutional limits on taxation as their form of imposed capitalism. Here are the words to describe fascistic capitalism:

Generals and admirals take power. They wipe out their leftist predecessors, exile opponents, jail dissident intellectuals, curb the trade-unions, and control the press and all political activity.

But, in this variant of market fascism, the military leaders stay out of the economy. *They* don't plan and don't take bribes. They turn over all economics to religious zealots – zealots whose religion is the laissez faire market, zealots who also take no bribes. (Opponents of the Chilean regime somewhat unfairly called this group 'the Chicago Boys,' in recognition that many of them had been trained or influenced by University of Chicago economists who favored free markets.)

Then the clock of history is turned back. The market is set free, and the money supply is strictly controlled. Without welfare transfer payments, workers must work or starve. Those unemployed now hold down the growth of the competitive wage rate. Inflation may well be reduced if not wiped out.

If the production index rises and foreign investments pour in, what is there to complain about? Political freedom aside, *there does tend to b a significant increase in the degree of inequality of incomes, consump tion, and wealth* under the archetypical pattern here envisaged.

EXAMPLE: The World Bank almanac shows superlative real growt for Brazil in the 1970s: but it also shows that the lowest 20 per cent o the population there receive only 2 per cent of total househol incomes, while the highest 20 per cent are getting 67 per cent – a unusual disparity.

What do Brazil, South Korea, Singapore, Mexico and Taiwan have i common? They are regarded as examples of *successfully developin countries*. Their manufacturing grows and captures markets in th affluent nations and the LDCs. But they are also *one-party politice systems, some of them outright dictatorships*.

I do not wish to leave you with the impression that fascistic capitalis is a good thing, or even that it will work. What do Mussolini, Nkruma Sukarno, Amin, Khan and the Shah have in common? All of them wei dictators who professed to make the trains run on time and to promot the growth of the GNP. For a time some of them even seemed to succee in their purpose, but I need to quote my textbook final words o imposed Capitalism:

> History records no known case where fascism succeeds, even on it own economic terms, for any sustained period. Alas, such system cannot evolve into normal democracies. Their business freedoms ar maintainable only by being *imposed* on the populistic voters. Th dictators dare not ease up on repression. They never know how muc dissent is being bottled up. As in Iran, it is only later that one learn how class divisions have been festering and widening.

X DREAMING

Personally, I must agree with Winston Churchill when he said tha although democracy is not a very good system, it is nevertheless bette than any other system. My dream is to make the mixed economy wor better.

We must try not to shrink the social pie and kill off its growth by ou struggles over the dividing of the pie. The goal is the old Marshallian on of using a cool head to realise the aspirations of a warm heart.

Is it utopian to retain and promote the *humane* qualities of the *mixe economy* while conserving the *efficiencies* of the market mechanism? Yes, it is utopian. But the rational pursuit of this goal provides our generation of economists with a worthy challenge.

REFERENCES

Keynes, J. M. (1930). 'Economic Possibilities for our Grandchildren', in *Essays in Persuasion* (London: Macmillan, 1933).
Schumpeter, J. A. (1942, 1947). *Capitalism, Socialism and Democracy* (New York: Harper & Row).
Samuelson, P. A. (1973). 'Worldwide Stagflation', reproduced in *Collected Scientific Papers* of Paul A. Samuelson, Vol. IV, H. Nagatani and K. Crowley (eds) (Cambridge, Mass.: MIT Press, 1977), Chapter 268, 801–7.
—— 1980. *Economics*, 11th edn (New York: McGraw-Hill), pp. 815–16.

ACKNOWLEDGEMENT

The editor and publishers are grateful to *Newsweek* for permission to quote the extract from 'Memories' by Paul Samuelson. Copyright 1969 by Newsweek, Inc.

Comment on Professor Samuelson's Paper: 'The World Economy at Century's End'

H. Giersch

Federal Republic of Germany

Professor Samuelson deserves the applause he has received for his address about Keynes, Schumpeter and 'The World Economy at Century's End'. However, my role is not to praise him, but to criticise. Let me try to discharge my duty:

  (i) by searching for a bias and for faults in Samuelson's picture; and
  (ii) by indicating where the picture does not fill the frame given by its title and the more general context of this congress' theme, 'Human Resources, Employment and Development'.

There are two main characters in the picture – Keynes and Schumpeter – and one favourite subject matter – the mixed economy. Samuelson is in sympathy with Keynes who, half a century ago, predicted the high standard of living – and the boredom – people would enjoy at the century's end in a Swedish-type society. The material foundation of this society is the mixed economy. Keynes himself seems to have given birth to it; at least he nursed it. For without the Keynesian Revolution there would not have been protection against deflation and persisting slump (p. 66), and the world would not have experienced the miracle decades of the 1950s and the 1960s (p. 66). As the mixed economy has humane qualities (p. 66) we are left with the impression that Keynes' real historical role was to be something like the alma mater (in its original sense) of the good society.

The second main character is Schumpeter, who happened to be Samuelson's teacher. He does not look like a good mother, but like an unsympathetic dominating father. Samuelson calls him cynical (p. 58, p. 66), schizophrenic (p. 60), and half a mountebank (p. 63). Methodologically, he must have been fairly authoritarian: with a wave of his hand he airily dismissed post-Keynesian apprehensions instead of invoking theoretical arguments (p. 62); his thought was confused (p. 68); and he broadened definitions when it suited him, for example the definition of a socialist to include Samuelson and others who are objective about capitalism (p. 68).

As a forecaster Schumpeter earns a C in Samuelson's eyes (p. 65) because he substantially underestimated the post-war performance of Germany and Japan, Sweden and Switzerland and of the whole world economy (p. 66). He even believed in Hitler's victory (p. 61)

Politically, he was a conservative (p. 70) and — if you read between Samuelson's lines — an advocate of the fascist solution (p. 75). Taken together this comes close to an overkill, cunningly hidden in a marvellous exposition devoted to the future of the world economy. Final judgement must be left to future historians, if not psychologists, of economic thought who have lower opportunity costs than we at this congress.

To turn to the subject matter, we note that Samuelson's main concern is the mixed economy, set in sharp contrast to Schumpeter's unfettered capitalism. For lack of definition, we have to gather that this type excludes both classical socialism and all countries where the market operates under the umbrella of a one-party dictatorship. It is unclear where he puts Mexico, but as to the OECD countries, they all seem to be included, with the possible exception of Yugoslavia. Samuelson's favourite example of a successful mixed economy is Sweden which is mentioned far more often than Keynes' own country. What is so exciting about the mixed economy, apart from its vitality which seems to contradict Schumpeter's horoscope or Hayek's horrorscope of an inevitable march into socialism? Is it an ongoing election campaign in the US or a hazardous Thatcher experiment in Britain? In my opinion the real issue of the mixed economy is — apart from stagflation — the unhappy choice between equity and efficiency, so aptly described by the late Arthur Okun.

If the characteristic feature of the mixed economy is the mix between market efficiency and a determined government policy in pursuit of equity and social security, I fail to see its relation to Keynes. Its roots can be traced further back to Bismarck's social security legislation of almost a hundred years ago and to those German economists who called their professional society founded in 1872 'Verein für Socialpolitik' or association for social policy. I also see a close link to the West German post-war concept of a 'social market economy'.

However, Samuelson is preoccupied with effective demand and with fiscal policy propelling the multiplier-accelerator mechanism. Thus private autonomous investment is left out of the picture, and the Schumpeterian entrepreneur, hardly alluded to by Samuelson, has no role to play as a driving force of economic development. I admit that the dynamic entrepreneur is now a rare animal, after more and more businessmen in mixed economies have become Keynesians waiting for the government to provide them with effective demand for induced investments; but the post-war economic miracle, at least of West Germany, mentioned by Samuelson, had a different engine. This

development is not at all miraculous when seen through Schumpeteria
rather than Keynesian glasses. If you want an explanation even mor
closely related to human resources than Schumpeter's you had better tr
to extract it from David MacClelland's pioneering book on th
'Achieving Society'.

As regards West Germany in the 1970's Samuelson maintains that h
performance was worse than that of the US. When on an earli
occasion he supported the point with statistics of industrial production
explained why this was not admissible in a period of accelerated decli
in the share of the industrial sector. Now the reference is to GDP. Her
the growth rate in the 1970s is indeed higher for the US (3.2 per cen
than for West Germany (2.8 per cent). However, West Germany clearl
outperformed the US in terms of GDP per capita, GDP per employe
and GDP per hour worked, not to mention the fantastic productivit
growth in West Germany's relatively shrinking industrial secto
Sweden, which receives so much praise for not slowing down the rate
growth of its social pie (p. 66) exceeded West Germany's post-wa
performance (p. 66) in no decade in terms of GDP, or GDP per capit
or GDP per person employed.

Sweden, which Samuelson believes to have shown annual produ
tivity improvement of 8 per cent, is in actual fact not advancing at
record pace. Trusting Denison's figures, we see Swedish productivit
growth from 1950 to 1973 below that of many other countries, thoug
above that of North America and the UK. From 1973 to 197
productivity growth in manufacturing was lower than before, b
particularly in Sweden; Sweden even fell behind Canada and the U
Only Britain was a worse performer than Sweden among the countri
selected by Denison (Denison, 1979, p. 146).

One of the central points in the present mixed economy debate is th
question whether government expenditure as a per cent of trend GD
will continue to rise, as it did until recently in all major OECD countrie
led by the Netherlands, the Scandinavian countries and the UK (OECI
June 1977, p. 211). The answer may well be yes, in accordance wit
Adolph Wagner's law formulated in 1861. This law is plausible to tho
who see Parkinson's law operating in 'bureaucracies without ban
ruptcy' and who observe how politicians compete for special groups
voters by making promises at taxpayers' expense.

But history has seen reverse swings, like the 'retreat from mercant
lism into laissez-faire in the nineteenth century' (Cairncross, 1976,
113), heralded by philosopher-economists of Scottish and Englis
origin. These intellectuals in Schumpeter's sense had a workab

alternative to government regulation – the market. This is why they were more successful in their drive towards a withering away of the state than Karl Marx and those who followed him in this respect. Intellectuals of the same spirit were at work in Prague in 1968. Economists seem to contribute to such swings with the fashions of the profession. When the market has a wide scope to operate we concentrate our efforts on supposed market failures, assuming a perfect government which ideally could do better. And when we accumulate experience under real world governments – mercantilist, fascist and socialist – we rediscover and preach the virtues of the market like those German economists around Walter Eucken who had opposed and yet survived Hitler. What Schumpeter possibly failed to see is that intellectuals tend to be dissidents in either polar system. Economists are intellectuals in the 'state versus market' controversy and are bound to overshoot as long as the profession is incapable of defining rules for the optimum division of labour between governments and markets which are sufficiently operational and can be applied in different socio-political circumstances.

As long as we have not done serious work in this field we have to rely on personal impressions. For the sake of further discussion let me draw on forty years experience in the German civil service and state the following presumptions:

(1) Civil servants are relatively efficient and usually do their best. Yet serious co-ordination inefficiencies do arise from overcentralisation, lack of relevant information in the bureaucratic communication system, institutional rigidity, and a systematic incapability of using and expanding the learning potential of the human resources employed.

(2) Most serious is the lack of rewards for economising, risk-taking and innovating. As a director of a government-financed and bureaucratically controlled research institute I have to spend most of my effort on maintaining and defending natural human motivations against external pressures to substitute control for confidence and regulation for incentives.

(3) Decentralisation of responsibility helps in many respects, but it cannot be tolerated in wide limits if the output is not subject to external evaluation and competition. Internal competition is merely a substitute; and it can mislead people who receive freedom for decision-making into becoming mere budget maximisers.

Fortunately for GNP growth, the government sector can rely upon the Central Statistical Office to estimate its output as equal to its input and to impute to its servants an annual productivity increase of 2 per cent or whatever the top secret guesstimate just may be. So much about X-efficiency in the public sector in countries like West Germany.

Outside the public sector, detailed regulations and controls have similar depressing effects on motivations and productivity improvements in the market. However, we in Germany observe many foreigners becoming petty entrepreneurs. The question of how they can cope with all the regulations formulated in an involved German that they can hardly read, let alone understand, has a plausible answer: they have the privilege of ignoring these regulations and of returning to southern Europe once they get into difficulties due to this ever-growing literature. Another striking observation is that the international sector of the West German economy which is exposed to the storms of Schumpeterian competition shows a much higher productivity growth than the overregulated and cartel-ridden domestic sector. Thus the open economy comes to the rescue of the mixed economy.

An alternative way of getting around the high state-content of the mixed economy is disloyalty: tax avoidance through shortening of the working week and retreat into tax-free activities during leisure time. Together with a subsidisation of search for employment by relatively high unemployment benefits and the pensioning off of the unemployed close to retirement age, this gives plausibility to presumptions that the modern mixed economy suffers from the emergence of a substantial underground economy. Those who want to learn more about this phenomenon are advised to study what is becoming known as Italy's 'new economic miracle'.

For Samuelson the real problem of the mixed economy is stagflation. My explanation for this disease is that politicians have been made to believe in the existence of a stable non-vertical Phillips curve. When unemployment is low they discover inflation, and when inflation is low they consider unemployment as public enemy number one. The outcome is a politically determined go and stop business cycle. Its go part (in terms of output) requires the existence of money illusion (supported if possible by exchange rate illusion) or adaptive expectations which bring about a time lag in the upward adjustment of wages and prices. An illusion which is thus exploited disappears. It then needs to be restored. This happens in recessions. The less effective this restoration, the greater must be the subsequent inflation if it is to produce the expected output effect. Thus, by walking up and down the

Phillips curve politicians shift it – and worsen the trade-off. The problem in my view requires extensive reform. The two conflicting targets of low unemployment and price level stability need a separate institution or instrument for each, and a division of labour between them that matches the norms of comparative advantage. This is not the place to describe the ideal solution; but some consensus societies (in the context of an open economy) seem to be on the right track when they gradually learn that there is more classical unemployment in this world than Keynesians believe and that such unemployment must be tackled on the wage front rather than by monetary acceleration.

Let me now talk about the world economy rather than Samuelson's paper. The main topic left out of his picture for the road to 1999 is the lack of productive jobs compared with the hundreds of millions of people in LDCs who need and deserve them. How can the advanced economies in the First World most effectively contribute to a mutually advantageous solution of this serious problem?

My answer, apart from development aid, is: make the mixed, advanced economy as open as possible for those LDCs that wish to take advantage of export-led growth and an international transfer of capital and knowledge. Resistance against liberal imports from countries with an abundant supply of labour is likely to be strong in countries where labour is well-organised and politically influential. This proposition is based on the Stolper–Samuelson theorem, on the existence of adjustment costs, and on the fact that governments usually have little manoeuvring room for paying adjustment assistance as a temporary device. The proposition is borne out by abundant experience. This seems to indicate that the real class conflict of our age is between labour in less developed countries and labour in advanced countries. The mixed economy may have humane qualities, as Samuelson emphasises, but its organisation in a nation state limits humanitarian activities essentially to compatriots, and perhaps even only to those who belong to pressure groups.

Unfortunately, the rich mixed economy solves some of its domestic problems at the expense of poorer countries in the Third World. Here is a short list of examples:

(1) A premature reduction of wage differentials – interindustrial, interregional and between unskilled and skilled workers – attempted in the name of equity, aggravates adjustment problems in structurally weak industries and regions, and contributes to heavy unemployment among youths, females and elderly

persons. To mitigate this effect on the poor at home, a system of import protection and subsidies is built up which largely discriminates against the poor abroad.

(2) Domestic labour unions, notably under co-determination, protest against direct investment in LDCs unless the investment is complementary to domestic labour and can be justified as securing domestic employment at higher real wages. This limits direct investment in LDCs to projects which are either sales-oriented or ensure cheap raw material supplies.

(3) High real wages for unskilled workers are a strong inducement to labour-augmenting innovations which raise the capital intensity built into the capital stock, including the capital intensity built into investment goods which are delivered to LDCs under development assistance programmes. The growing unemployment in the world economy has thus little to do with effective demand, but very much with technology and capital shortage.

(4) Artificially low energy prices, notably in the US, maintained under populist pressures, worsen the position of oil-importing LDCs.

(5) Government deficits in advanced countries, often recommended for preventing domestic unemployment, have a crowding-out effect not only on domestic firms but also on foreign firms and governments, including governments of LDCs.

In search of a common cause for such malfunctions, I dare to submit a hypothesis that could help us to understand, if not predict or prevent, some likely developments in the world economy during the next two decades:

(1) The tendency to overvalue present goods relative to future goods (observed by Böhm-Bawerk) leads to an increased shortage of capital unless the real rate of interest is allowed to be positive and high enough.

(2) Under the impact of policies devised to fight classical unemployment by Keynesian methods, the mixed economy shows a tendency to depress the real rate of interest, sometimes below zero.

(3) Mankind tends to overvalue human resources not only in relation to physical capital but also in relation to natural resources, including exhaustible raw material deposits and in relation to human capital.

(4) Once the shortage of natural resources and of capital exceeds threshold levels, human resources will accept, although reluct-

antly, a devaluation. This will be felt as a crisis. It will probably last until mankind has adjusted to a sufficiently high real rate of interest on both capital and exhaustible resources.

(5) The mixed economy in advanced countries is abused to prevent market forces from enforcing quick adjustments to changes in the world economy. The main reason is that the objective of social justice is vague and that, in the absence of generally accepted norms, traditional relative prices and traditional income differentials are often taken as the best possible approximation. This social conservatism is likely to lead to increasing protection against LDCs. The Stolper–Samuelson theorem demonstrates how the relative value of human resources can be maintained in advanced countries, albeit at the expense of LDCs and world welfare.

(6) In advanced countries, such protectionism reduces economic growth by slowing down structural change; and in LDCs it strengthens political pressures in favour of delinking and import-substitution policies. Defensive investments in advanced countries defeat LDC attempts at earning the foreign exchange needed for job-creating investments. Taken together this is likely to exacerbate the capital shortage and unemployment in the world economy in this century.

Let me conclude on an optimistic note. Like Samuelson, I have a dream. It is about the open rather than the mixed economy. To be specific, I shall formulate several wishes addressed to the European Community of which my country of citizenship is a member.

First: replace the Common Agricultural Policy by a system of income subsidies so as to end the vicious circle of producing, protecting, storing or dumping that arises from excessive 'target prices', 'intervention prices' and 'threshold prices' (Cairncross, Giersch, Lamfalussy, Petrilli and Uri, 1974, pp. 91–115). The waste which the mixed economy produces in this area, while large parts of the world suffer from starvation, is a bad precedent and a human tragedy.

Second: enlarge the Community, but make sure that the new entrants will support commercial openness as if they were still excluded.

Third: make a unilateral and irreversible pledge that all imports will be fully liberalised from duties and controls in a series of steps before the end of this century.

Fourth: member countries should be induced to cut all permanent subsidies in a parallel series of steps in order to obtain financial means for granting adjustment assistance on a temporary basis; capital losses, however, need to be compensated for only if and to the extent that windfall profits have been subject to taxes and provide the financial means.

Fifth: capital outflows will follow free commodity imports once domestic entrepreneurs have learned that it is both possible and cheaper to serve the domestic market for standardised products by producing in countries where labour is abundant. LDCs wishing to participate in this resource transfer should be invited to form investment agreements which clearly define the frontiers between government and enterprises and which give assurances against whatever political risks are seen as an impediment.

Sixth: technology follows investment and trade, but rich EC countries can do much to encourage the export of investment goods which incorporate technologies appropriate for LDCs. Fears about unemployment in rich countries can easily be dispelled by demonstrating the vast demand for investment goods that is bound to develop once LDCs can earn more foreign exchange and become viable capital importers. There is no Keynesian liquidity trap in the Third World.

Seventh: rich EC countries which import more and more standardised Heckscher–Ohlin goods and will also have to pay relatively more for resource-based Ricardo goods can maintain their position on the world income scale by concentrating resources on the research and the development of new and better products which, in honour of Samuelson's teacher, I like to call Schumpeter goods.

Eighth: the developing advanced rich economy must be open vis-à-vis the future as well as vis-à-vis less advanced countries. Openness vis-à-vis the future requires a free market in ideas as well as in goods. This practically excludes fascism and other forms of dictatorship. Hence there is no fascist solution that could be imagined for a Schumpeterian economy, whatever Schumpeter may have thought a couple of decades ago.

Ninth: perhaps the most important good for the world economy is good money, money with a fairly stable value in terms of goods and services. The dollar, after having been used to produce the environment for the miracle decade of the 1960s, no longer qualifies for that role. Those central banks in Europe which produce close competitors to the dollar should quickly learn how to become the supplier of the *n* currency and how to earn the compensating seignorage gain.

Tenth: Europe will remain one of the three centres of the world economy outside Comecon. Having largely caught up with the US in the last three decades, the strong countries in the European Community should feel responsible for a Community policy that would help other countries to catch up with them. It is in this way that international income differentials can be reduced in a worldwide positive-sum game.

Although these wishes are addressed to policy-makers I am not without hope. This hope is based on the belief that people in a society which is open vis-à-vis the rest of the world and open vis-à-vis the future cannot but learn from failures and success.

REFERENCES

Cairncross, A. (1976). 'The Market and the State', in T. Wilson and A. S. Skinner (eds), *The Market and the State, Essays in Honour of Adam Smith* (Oxford: Clarendon Press), pp. 113–34.

Cairncross, A., H. Giersch, A. Lamfalussy, G. Petrilli and P. Uri, (1974). *Economic Policy for the European Community, The Way Forward* (London and Basingstoke: Macmillan).

Denison, E. F. (1979). *Accounting for Slower Economic Growth – The United States in the 1970s* (The Brookings Institution, Washington DC).

MacClelland, D. (1961). *The Achieving Society* (Princeton, NJ: Van Nostrand).

McCracken, P. *et al.* (1977). 'Towards Full Employment and Price Stability', a report to the OECD by a group of independent experts (Paris: OECD Publications).

KIELER ARBEITSPAPIERE (KIEL WORKING PAPERS)

95. *B. Fischer, E. Gerken, U. Hiemenz*, Growth and Employment in Mexico – A Quantitative Analysis of Policies. Kiel, November 1979. 86 S.
96. *J. Roth*, Reallöhne und Beschäftigung in einer offenen expandierenden Wirtschaft – Eine Modellskizze. Kiel, November 1979. 41 S.
97. *W. Prewo*, Ocean Fishing: Economic Efficiency and the Law of the Sea. Kiel, December 1979. 43 S.
98. *P. Nunnenkamp*, Zur Auslandsverschuldung der Entwicklungsländer – Ausmaß und Ursachen. Kiel, January 1980. 62 S.
99. *F. Wolter*, The Impact of Manufactured Imports from Developing Countries in the Federal Republic of Germany. Kiel, February 1980. 34 S.
100. *A. Erdilek*, The Direct Foreign Investment Process in Turkish Manufacturing. Kiel, March 1980. 134 S.
101. *K. -O. Junginger-Dittel and Th. Mayer*, Producer Income Instability and Farmers' Risk Response: The Case of Major Kenyan Export Crops. Kiel, March 1980. 135 S.
102. *R. J. Langhammer*, Multilateral Trade Negotiations among Less Developed Countries. A New Field for the GATT. Kiel, March 1980, 18 S.
103. *Th. Mayer and B. Fisher*, On the Structuralist View of Inflation in some Latin-American Countries: A Reassessment. Kiel, April 1980. 19 S.

104. *R. Fürstenberg and J. Scheide*, Ansätze zur Inflationsprognose. Ein Beitrag über die voraussichtliche Entwicklung in der Bundesrepublik. Kiel, May 1980. 27 S.
105. *K. -O. Junginger-Dittel*, Marketing Boards für Agrarexportgüter in Entwicklungsländern. Kiel, May 1980. 48 S.
106. *R. Fürstenberg*, Monetary Policy in Switzerland – The Performance During the Seventies. Kiel, June 1980. 26 S.
107. *P. Nunnenkamp*, Neuere Formen des Protektionismus in Entwicklungsländern – Eine Bestandsaufnahme. Kiel, July 1980. 41 S.
108. *H. Weise*, Mischfinanzierung als Beitrag zur internationalen Entwicklungsfinanzierung. Kiel, July 1980. 60 S.
109. *Th. Mayer*, Zum Zusammenhang zwischen Exporterlösschwankungen und Investitionsgüterimporten in ausgewählten Entwicklungsländern. Kiel, August 1980. 21 S.
110. *H. Giersch*, Comment on Paul A. Samuelson's Paper: The World Economy at Century's End. Kiel, August 1980. 14 S.

Comments on Professor Samuelson's Paper: 'The World Economy at Century's End'

Tigran S. Khachaturov

USSR

Professor Samuelson begins his paper with the question: from whom could he learn to discern the road ahead until the century's end? From a few of prominent prophets, as he calls them, he chooses Keynes and especially Schumpeter, and, as though with their eyes, he tries to look at the future. The choice of Keynes and Schumpeter certainly is not ill-considered. Their views exerted influence on the formation of his own theoretical position, which he himself later calls a theory of neo-classical synthesis.

I have read, with expectation of something fresh, what the author has said about Keynes's forecast, made before the great depression, of the rates of economic growth for the future. But in fact it turns out that Keynes has simply assumed that if the average growth rate can be 2 per cent at compound interest over the next hundred years, then the GNP will increase several times. In the paper there are also many references to Schumpeter; for example, his second axiom on the political instability of capitalism, recollections of his discussion with Sweezy under the Leontieff chairmanship in Harvard on the future of capitalism, his published American Economic Association address on 'The March to Socialism'.

It is well known that Schumpeter was not very friendly towards my country, but I learn something new about his attitude from the paper. Professor Samuelson tells us that Schumpeter was saddened by the expectation that the Soviet Union would be the true victor of the war. In Schumpeter's view, writes Samuelson, 'we [that is the US] had been engaged with the wrong ally in fighting the wrong enemy'. It is sad that Schumpeter was of such a reactionary (or even worse) opinion.

These remarks in the paper bear little relation to the subject of our congress and even to the title of the paper, which is in many respects most interesting and written with wit and humour.

I think, however, that it will be useful to continue and develop some of Samuelson's arguments in the section of his paper on 'the miraculous mid-century sprint'. It is important to establish more exactly the causes of the rapid economic growth in capitalist countries during this period. It seems to me that, in addition to certain initial impulses, such as the Marshall plan, the abolition of feudal obligations in Japan, and some decrease of military burdens in the developed countries, a very important contribution to the increased economic growth came from rapid technological progress. In the 1950s and 1960s there wa widespread expansion of such innovations as, for example, computeris ation, use of atomic energy, television, space flights, new syntheti materials, the transplant of human organs, and so on. These innovation were made possible by the achievements of science in the precedin years, and some of them by intensive research during the war. In th 1970s the situation changed, and the rates of growth were approximatel halved. There were several reasons for this slow down. Briefly overproduction in developing capitalist countries, growing competitio in international markets, stagflation and increasing unemployment Also very important was the slow down of technological progress. It i difficult to recall now any new innovations, any new achievements o science and technology, which were comparable with the innovations o the middle of the century. Unfavourable to economic growth were th worsened situation with regard to natural resources, the increase o expenditure for the protection of the environment, and finally th deplorable military expenditures.

We cannot yet foresee how and when all of these obstacles t economic growth will be overcome. Thus we can hardly expect th growth rate of capitalist countries to be more than 2–3 per cent down t the end of the century.

There is at the same time a slow down in the economies of socialis countries. This is due to the expiration of the extensive factors in growth These factors are not infinite. The rate of population growth ha decreased and the labour force in the sphere of material production ha stabilised or even decreased. A rise in population is now possible mainl through the rise of labour productivity. The best natural resources ar becoming more and more exhausted; new resources require larg amounts of investments; it is therefore necessary to achieve mor effective use of raw materials. There is also the necessity of strengthenin the weak and outdated infrastructure, and of ensuring the protection o the environment, among other things. The transition to intensive form of development requires considerable expenditure, widespread organis ational measures, changes of traditional ideas, the revision of theorie and thus rather long periods of time.

Socialist countries have large reserves of further growth, thanks to th advantages of a planning system which makes the full use of thes reserves possible. It is necessary to put them in action. From the lates statistical report of the Central Statistical Board of the USSR, for th first half of this year, it is possible to see that industrial production ha increased by 4.2 per cent over last year, and labour productivity in industry by 3.2 per cent.

I believe that an annual growth of 4.2 per cent is the real minimal perspective of development of Soviet industry during the transition period down to the end of the century.

Allow me now to say something on the main subject of the congress – on human resources – as the French say: *Revenons à nos moutons*. First a few words about the so-called population explosion. It is usually interpreted as a negative phenomenon, encouraging grave fears for the fate of further development, because of scarcity of resources. But as a matter of fact the increase of world population represents a much more complex phenomenon.

The causes of it have positive character and bear witness to the achievements of human society: acceleration of population growth is a consequence of the decrease of the death rate as a result of scientific progress, improvement of medical services, the elimination of contagious diseases, and economic growth. At the same time, in a majority of countries the birth rate either remains at its previous level or is going down slightly, though much more slowly than the death rate. This means that population growth is the result of the improvement of people's health and well-being, representing one of the achievements of human civilisation. From the point of view of the progress of human society, the increase of population should in itself be appraised positively. Population growth can be seen to be the prerequisite of labour force growth – and in certain conditions, given improvement of the educational system, it is the precondition for creating and expanding the necessary amount of skilled manpower. This in turn is the factor causing the increase of production which is necessary to the welfare of society.

It is clear, however, that not only the absolute number of population but also the appropriate ratio of the figure to the level and rate of growth of production are of great importance. It is necessary to create a sufficient number of jobs to balance the growing supply in the labour market and secure full employment of the population. In the USSR, for several decades, the problem of shifting the labour force from agriculture to industry, of building up the transportation system, of securing higher skills, and the creation of an increasing number of jobs to absorb the growing population have been successfully solved and have provided full employment of the whole population (in the USSR unemployment had already been eliminated by 1930). There is no unemployment in any of the socialist countries.

Facts have shown that the elimination of unemployment is quite

feasible in the actual social circumstances. The growth of the unemplo
ment rate in developing countries from 25 per cent in 1970 to 30 per ce
in 1980 cannot possibly be considered to be an inevitable result
population growth in itself. Production growth creates the necessa
conditions for accumulation, on the basis of which it is possible
augment the capital investments and to use them to create new jobs.
this connection, raising labour productivity is of great importanc
Between 1928 and 1979 labour productivity in industry in the USSR h
risen twenty-five times.

Insufficient increase of labour productivity in developing countrie
combined with unemployment and a low rate of accumulation, may lea
to an unfavourable balance of production growth and increase
population, if as a result the number of consumers rises more rapid
than the number of producers.

Under such circumstances the possibility of reducing birth rates
developing countries, as a consequence of the advance of education a
the standard of culture resulting from the decrease in population grow
rates, should be taken into consideration. According to some evidenc
literacy alone considerably reduces the birth rate. In a number
countries it has been noted that the fertility rate of women who ha
completed elementary and secondary education (in Ghana, for instanc
has been reduced significantly. Education gives women access
vocational training, helps to raise the standard of living, creat
incentives to diminish the family size. Moreover, the improvement
nutrition itself leads to a lowering of fertility. According to the theory
demographic transition, many societies are moving from both high bir
and high death rates, first to high birth rates and low death rates, ar
then to both low birth and low death rates. The demographic theo
formulated as long ago as 1929 is apparently justified for the develope
countries, but needs further examination of its applicability for t
developing countries.

For several decades past the process of raising the standard ar
quality of life in the developing countries has unquestionably been goir
on. But this phenomenon is not going on at the desired pace. Th
amount of skilled manpower in developing countries is constant
growing, the number of people learning at schools is continually risin
But much remains to be done to spread even elementary educatio
During the last ten years, the proportion of the illiterate has decrease
from 44 to approximately 33 per cent, but their absolute number ha
grown.

One of the most important practical questions for the next stages the development of human society appears to be the provision of our planet's growing population with food. Analysis of the statistical data for the world as a whole shows that even during the last ten years, with accelerated world population growth, its rate of increase has not been faster than the growth of food production.

A fall of agricultural production per capita should, however, be noted in some countries of Africa and Asia. In these countries, the aggravation of food shortages and even famine, is quite likely. In other developing countries, agricultural production per capita remains at the same level as before. In the majority of Latin-American countries, it is appreciably increasing. As a whole, until now per capita production of such foodstuffs as wheat, rice, maize, soya beans, sugar-cane and cotton for the world as a whole, and per capita meat production in such countries as Argentina, Brazil, Australia and New Zealand has substantially grown.

One should bear in mind the continued availability of sizable land reserves, assuming the implementation of land-reclamation measures, making it possible to double or even treble the area of arable land and further increase crops. But one must remember that the output of intensive agriculture demands significant expenditures for land reclamation, fertilisers, agricultural machinery, energy, and other inputs, which result in raising the costs of the output and its price. Here there arises the question of the comparative costs of bringing new arable lands into production and the costs of increasing yields. This analysis makes it possible to determine how far expansionary projects, if carried out, will justify their costs, and at what time they should be undertaken.

To form any judgement regarding the world's perspective social development one needs not only to know the total world potentialities but also to consider their differentiation in terms of separate climatic zones and different groups of countries. The most important problem continues to be the gap between the developed and developing nations and the ways to reduce it.

It is notorious that the ten-year programme of 'third world development' which was carried out under the aegis of UNO has not justified the expectations built on it. Possibly the help of the developed countries to the developing countries can be no more than a push – a fairly powerful push, certainly – in the direction of economic growth – so that the growth will be achieved at the expense of the inner resources of each country. The experience of a number of socialist countries, and above all that of the USSR, should be taken into account. In the USSR, down to the moment of revolution in 1917, agriculture was predominant,

industry was ravaged, it was impossible to rely on foreign investment
thus industrialisation had to be accomplished by means of internal
accumulations; full employment was achieved, poverty was abolished

The developing countries are nowadays in a far better position than
the socialist world was at the beginning of its industrialisation period
Physical conditions in many developing countries are in good shape; the
utilisation of the gifts of nature reduces the necessary expenditure of
labour. Sizable natural resources exist, serving at present as basic
sources of many types of raw materials for the developed countries
Exporting these types of raw materials at suitable prices may substan
tially further the development of the countries' exports.

The utilisation of the internal potentials of the developing nations
requires considerable effort on their part. The development of education
and culture, the training of their own specialists, are of the greatest
importance. Equally important for the creation of the preconditions of
economic growth is that the developing countries should take steps to
improve some elements and create other elements of infrastructure
necessary for expanding employment.

It is necessary to establish, probably under the aegis of UNO, a system
for planning the developing nation's resources, if only in the form of
indicative planning. This will facilitate the most effective allocation of
human and material resources in these countries and co-ordinate their
mutual activities. The introduction of a system of efficient economic
information about the development of these countries, based on
comparable accepted definitions, should be an important prerequisite of
this process. Information of such a type will show up the results of the
measures taken, their effectiveness and the need for changes and will
contribute to the efficient solution of the most important tasks of long
term human development.[1]

---

[1] [*Editorial Note.* The addresses of Dr Flores de la Pěna and Lord Kaldor in
the Final Sessions (pp. 131–40 below) in effect continue the debate on
Professor Paul Samuelson's paper.]

4 Economic Development and Human Resources: Japan's Experience

Shigeto Tsuru

JAPAN

I INTRODUCTORY

Japan commenced her deliberate efforts at modernisation in 1868, the year of so-called Meiji Restoration, and it is generally agreed that by the end of the nineteenth century she had succeeded in entering the stage of sustained economic growth. The first decade after the Restoration was naturally characterised by the storm and strain of the major political and social transformation from a typically feudal society into a highly nationalistic capitalism. The last of civil strife, accompanied by serious inflation, was not put down until 1877; and it was only after the successful monetary stabilisation achieved through the Matsukata Deflation of 1881–85 that the economy got into the stride of cumulative growth. In other words, the last quarter of the last century may be said to be crucial for the purpose of analysing factors of the economic development of Japan. This essay, therefore, focuses its attention mainly on that period.

II THE NATURE OF REQUIREMENTS FOR HUMAN RESOURCES

In terms of economic systems, Japan's economic development was essentially *capitalistic*. In other words, the unit of economic activities was private capital under the control of entrepreneurs bent on maximising private gains. Price mechanism reigned in the circumstance of ever-evolving money economy; and free competition was the rule either at home or vis-à-vis foreign economies. And industrialisation progressed against this background. To this, however, the qualification has to be added immediately that the state played an important role, especially during the first decade after the Restoration – more or less a matter of necessity in view of Japan's attempt at forcing the pace in her struggle to create a viable capitalism as a latecomer. There was then no such thing as foreign aid, either financial or technical. As a matter of fact, the leaders of the country then held an attitude of suspicion of any foreign capital and deliberately shunned borrowing from abroad. Besides, by the terms of the treaties of commerce signed with the United States and other countries before the Restoration, Japan was not permitted to levy more than 5 per cent *ad valorem* duties on her imports, and it was extremely difficult for her to nurse infant industries along. Thus in more ways than one the state came to the assistance of private enterprises, or took its own initiative in setting up a new industry or a new enterprise subsequently to be handed over to private firms.

The nature of requirements for human resources, then, has to be discussed in the light of the peculiar circumstances which characterised the economic development of Japan. For any case of modernisation it may be said that the major categories of human resources that are required are:

   (i) labour suitable for work in modern factories;
  (ii) men with modern technical training;
 (iii) teachers;
 (iv) efficient administrators.

To this has to be added, in the case of capitalistic development in particular, another category (v) risk-taking entrepreneurs. So far as these requirements in general terms are concerned, Japan shares the common experience of many other countries in the course of development. However, once we go a step further in spelling out the concrete list of requirements for the case of Japan, we realise immediately that additional constraints are dictated by the unique features of the country's development.

Thus, for example, it was not sufficient for Japan simply to create a labour force adapted for work in modern factories. This in itself was not an easy task in as much as typical workers in the pre-modern period were not accustomed to 'sell their labour power for wages' but were usually family workers on the farm or apprentices or journeymen in guilds. The factory discipline was something new for them and urban living was often a strange experience. In addition, in the case of Japan, it was essential that such a labour force should be acquired at an exceptionally cheap price. Otherwise, it was obvious that new Japanese industries could not compete with imported goods from advanced industrialised countries.

In a greater or lesser degree, each one of the major categories listed above had its additional constraints which were inextricably related to the peculiarity of Japan's experience. To enumerate these requirements and constraints is, however, an exercise which we can do by hindsight. In point of fact, at the time, things happened with less awareness of what was going on; and in a sense it may be truer to say that, aside from the nationalistic orientation which the Meiji leaders possessed, various forces, each motivated by its own purpose or interest, impinged and reacted upon each other to produce the results which are now history.

III HOW WERE THE REQUIREMENTS FILLED?

Table 4.1 gives the distribution of the gainfully employed in major industry sectors for a number of benchmark years, 1872 being the first year for which such statistics are available and 1920 being the first census year. It is clearly shown in the table that, although the weight of the primary sector remained high until the end of the last century, a steady rise in the relative importance of the secondary sector can be observed during the crucial period of Japan's economic development.

A more detailed picture for the manufacturing sector is shown in Table 4.2 where the amount of labour employed in 'factories' is given by industrial subsectors for 1882 and 1892. Statistics are only roughly comparable between the two years since the criterion for coverage differs. But the general impression one gains from the table is likely to be not too wide of the mark. As might be expected, textiles predominate, with silk-reeling occupying more than a half of the total for manufacturing in 1882 and cotton-spinning gaining rapidly from 1363 to 29,103 in ten years. Table 4.2 also reveals a characteristic feature of factory employment in those days, that is the reliance on the labour of women and children, especially in the textile industry. In silk-reeling, for example, almost one-fifth of factory labour in 1882 was fifteen-year-olds or younger and among the rest nine-tenths were women. Cotton-

TABLE 4.1   GAINFULLY EMPLOYED BY MAJOR INDUSTRY
SECTORS, 1872–1920
(in 000s)

	1872	1880	1900	1920
Population	34,940	36,868	44,231	55,963
Age 15–59	21,107	21,564	25,893	30,950
Active labour force	19,063	19,542	24,768	27,263
Primary sector	14,702	16,076	17,331	14,848
Secondary sector	701	1,105	2,929	4,593
Tertiary sector	1,862	2,361	4,508	7,822
Unclassified	1,798			
Percentage of each sector to				
total active labour force	%^{a}	%	%	%
Primary sector	85.2	82.2	70.0	54.5
Secondary sector	4.0	5.7	11.8	16.8
Tertiary sector	10.8	12.1	18.2	28.7

^{a} Percentages are taken to the total excluding 'unclassified'.

Source: The 1872 figures are based on the data compiled by the Registration Bureau of the Ministry of the Interior; others are the estimates by Kazushi Ohkawa *et al., The Growth Rate of the Japanese Economy since 1878* (1957).

spinning does not present such a striking picture in 1882; but as that industry grew, the degree of dependence on women's labour increased, and in 1892 the ratio of male to female was exactly one to three.

In other words, if we can say that industrialisation spearheaded Japan's economic development and that textiles were the leading industry, we must add that young women, wherever they came from, constituted a major category of the new labour force, filling a most important requirement of the time.

1   MOBILISATION OF FEMALE LABOUR

Among the industries on which the Restoration government laid special emphasis, silk-reeling was the earliest, in view of its importance as a major export industry. To expand the production of raw silk and to improve its quality as a standardised commodity was a matter of absolute necessity for the country, suddenly thrown open for external commerce and needing an exportable good of some size and potentiality. Here was an industry which, during the Tokugawa period, had operated on the rural periphery, catering to a small domestic market, and which was now called upon to meet and satisfy the discriminating

TABLE 4.2   LABOUR EMPLOYED IN MANUFACTURING
'FACTORIES', 1882 AND 1892
(persons)

	Total	1882			1892
		Age 16 or older Male	Female	Age 15 or younger	
Textiles	45,623	4,510	32,846	8,267	123,276
Silk-reeling	37,452	2,755	27,702	6,995	68,783
Cotton-spinning	1,363	472	785	106	29,103
Weaving	6,808	1,283	4,359	1,166	23,176
Others					2,214
Food-processing	229	196	33	—	8,164
Metals and machinery	3,381	2,988	117	276	6,990
Metals	—	—	—	—	1,974
Machinery	—	—	—	—	1,944
Shipbuilding	—	—	—	—	3,072
Chemicals	7,459	4,343	2,069	1,047	27,483
Other manufacturing	1,916	1,510	231	175	14,381
TOTAL	58,608	13,547	35,296	9,765	180,294

Note: The 1882 survey was for those establishments which called themselves a 'factory' (*kōjō*) whereas the 1892 survey was for those establishments with a capital of 1000 *yen* or more.

Source: *Statistical Yearbook of Japan*, Nos 4 and 13.

demand of foreign buyers. Thus, a metamorphosis of the industry had to be guided by the government, which as early as 1870 invited a Swiss specialist in order to introduce the western technique of reeling. Small manufactory-type establishments, which had been the rule earlier, had to be transformed to a machine-operating factory size; in 1872 the government decided to establish a model plant at Tomioka with machinery imported from France which made use of steam power. But the difficulties encountered in manning this Tomioka plant were characteristic of the transition period.

At first the government attempted to recruit volunteers from the surrounding region; but 'since in those days steam-powered machines were never seen in rural regions, rumours spread that the smoke emanating from the plant would be poisonous or that there was some mechanism designed to suck living blood from working girls,[1] and there

[1] Tahachi Yajima, *Kanra Sangyō Sōdan (Various Stories on Industries in Kanra County)*, 1909, pp. 32–3.

were few who responded to the government call. In the end, therefore, the authorities fell back upon the resort of drafting daughters of the former retainers of the Tokugawa government and obtained slightly over one hundred hands. This was not enough and finally, Mr Odaka, who was administratively responsible for the model plant, offered his own daughter (thirteen years-old) as a factory hand and suggested to other civil servants that they should emulate him. It was only thus that upwards of 400 girls could be assembled for the plant. Typical among them was Hideko Yokota (1857–1929), a *samurai*'s daughter, whose *Tomioka Diaries*, posthumously published, relates with unusual vividness the atmosphere and day-to-day operation of the model plant under the guidance of five Frenchmen. The girls trained at the Tomioka plant were subsequently dispersed to different localities to serve as 'instructresses' in newly established modern plants, most of which were financed by government rehabilitation loans and silk-merchants' capital. Hideko, for example, returned to her native town of Matsushiro after sixteen months at Tomioka and worked as an 'instructress' at the age of seventeen at a new plant in Rokku. There, as she relates, she had to fight against the irrational prejudices of the older men in the plant,[2] and even the general hostility of the public outside the plant. The spirit at Tomioka, Rokku and such other places in those days was such that the girls were made to believe that it was an honour to be able to work there, and the matter of wages was considered beneath their dignity.[3]

It cannot be doubted that the initial efforts by the government to introduce the modern western technique of silk-reeling bore fruit, especially by the creation of a fair-sized number of 'instructresses' who, born of good family and having intelligence, spread the technique with confidence and zeal. But the model plant stage itself was a short-lived episode. As the export demand for silk expanded rapidly, the number of reeling plants increased by leaps and bounds, and the manner of their

[2] At one time, older men of the plant suggested that boiling cocoons at a stronger heat would result in better silk, at which Hideko protested. In the experimental spirit she learned at Tomioka, she proposed to reel out two kinds of product – one according to the older men's suggestion and the other her own, and ship them to Yokohama to have assessment made. She won in the end.

[3] Hideko's parents, for example, would not permit her to receive monetary remuneration for her work at Rokku; and when 5 *yen* was proffered by the company at the year-end of 1874, they bought the equivalent sum of dried mushrooms and gourd noodles and presented them to the girl's dormitory of the plant. Hideko had hoped at the time that at least a part of the money could be her own for the purchase of something for herself; and she wrote afterwards that for the rest of her life she repented her selfish thought of the occasion.

operation became increasingly more business-like. The turning point was around 1876, after which it became out of question to draw the labour supply from the proud, well-to-do families of the ex-*samurai* class. As, one after another, reeling plants came to be established, usually on the periphery of a rural community near the supply source of cocoons, the labour force needed came at first from among women of nearby regions; but they soon faced a shortage, in as much as many of these women were from farms where their help was badly needed, especially in busy seasons. Recruiting from a wider region became a necessity; and once this became the rule, the natural choice was for unmarried young girls, and since for them commuting was out of question, dormitories had to be built.

Although recruiting did not become any easier as time went on, what with the competition from the spinning industry, the treatment of the girls employed showed no sign of progress in respect of civilised care. The most difficult job for the recruiting scouts was persuading the girls' parents. In Gumma district a three-to-five-year term contract was usually offered, with the provision of board and room for the girl *plus* ten to fifteen *yen* cash payment, of which one-third was an advance. For destitute farmers who were in debt, this advance lump sum constituted an attraction and the advance ratio could be adjusted by the scouts to fit the case. In Nagano district, on the other hand, the daily wage system was more common, the rate ranging from around 5 *sen* to anywhere below 15 during the decade of the 1880s. It was customary, however, to combine a piece rate with this, involving a rather severe penalty deduction for inferior performance. One kilogram of rice cost 6 *sen* in those days (or 9 *sen* for one *sho*); and the bare subsistence used to be represented by 1.5 kilograms of rice per day. Thus, whatever method of payment was used, the wage income of these girls took the character either of supplementing the family income of the poorest class or of lightening the burden on the family to the extent they could be fed outside.

The problem with which the cotton-spinning industry was faced was no easier. With the opening of ports, cotton products poured into Japan, forming more than one-third of total imports during the first decade of the Restoration. The government naturally felt a strong need to create an import-substituting industry in this sphere, and hastened to introduce the western technique. Here again, a number of model plants were set up. Success, however, was slow to come, partly because the government harboured the mixed purpose of making the cotton-spinning industry a sphere for rehabilitation of the declassé warriors.

The unit of operation thus tended to be small, with a 2000-spindle plant the standard, and plants were scattered all over the country. Inexperience in handling the machines caused frequent stoppages; and the best they could produce was No 20 count yarns, which were no match against cheaper, better quality imports and competed rather with native cottage industry products.

A new turn came only in 1883, when the Osaka Spinning Company, with a capacity of more than 10,000 spindles, commenced operation with two twelve-hour shifts a day. The lesson was immediately learned; and as the Matsukata deflation ended in 1885, the industry, no longer concerned either with the social problem of rehabilitation of the declassé warriors or with the earlier official policy of building a plant near the site of native raw cotton supply, gathered momentum with tremendous speed. The first batch of exports of cotton yarns was shipped out in 1890, and by 1897 Japan's exports of yarns surpassed her imports of the same commodity.

The labour required for modern spinning mills was initially recruited more or less in the same manner as for the silk-reeling plants. Since the earlier 2000-spindle unit plants were intended partly for the rehabilitation of the feudal retainer class, their wives and daughters or persons introduced by them were given priority. But once the industry stood on its own feet and started expanding, the logic of economic calculation began having its sway. Since the size of a plant was bigger than in the case of silk-reeling plant, the recruitment policy also had to be better organised, and it was especially characteristic of the spinning industry that a natural calamity, like a big earthquake or a flood, was taken advantage of to persuade the destitute victims to sign an indenture for their daughters. Thus at the time of the Nobi earthquake of 1891, a host of scouts swarmed upon Gifu prefecture, as was also the case in Wakayama when there was a big flood in 1889. The need for recruiting was doubly felt on account of a high turnover, due probably to the unexpectedly harsh working conditions in spinning mills. At Kanegabuchi Spinning Mill, for example, there were on average 400 men and 1500 women workers during 1891, but within that year 312 men and 1001 women newly hired and 224 men and 1064 women left.[4] The competition in scouting naturally became more severe as the time went on, and numerous incidents of the kidnapping of skilled workers are recorded. At the same time, employers began to take stricter measures to

---

[4] See Mikio Sumiya, *Nihon Chinrōdōshi Ron (History of Wage Labour in Japan)*, 1955, p. 193.

isolate their employees from outside contacts, as if to confess that they were actually paying less to the girls than the market forces would have indicated.

By the 1890s cotton-spinning became, after silk-reeling, the second biggest industry in Japan, employing (in 1896) 52,582 workers of whom 32,689 were women, mostly young girls aged between 15 and 20. The average daily wage rate was 17.10 *sen* for males and 8.21 *sen* for females in 1889 and rose to 19.42 *sen* for males and 11.36 *sen* for females by 1896.[5] Although the wage differential by sex narrowed slightly between these dates, the three-to-two ratio was not broken until prosperity came with the First World War.

2 'FROM STATUS TO CONTRACT'

The account, given above, of the emergence of modern textile plants and of the manner in which their labour requirements were filled already gives a glimpse of the transition 'from status to contract' which was characteristic of the period of early Meiji years. The conditions of employment of Hideko Yokota, a daughter of the feudal ruling class, still retained the 'status' aspect, which gradually gave way to a type of employer–employee relationship which was a compromise between the tradition and the logic of capitalism.

The transition 'from status to contract', of course, was most drastic for the *samurai* class and sufficiently serious for guild craftsmen. How these two classes of people were rehabilitated and reorganised in the new society is a major problem of research which is indispensable, as a background, in answering the question on human resources and economic development of Japan.

It is estimated that there were approximately 400,000 families with 1.9 million members who belonged to the feudal *samurai* class in 1868, roughly 6 per cent of the population. They, after all, constituted the élite class under the Shogunate regime, having received the best education and being accustomed to taking leadership in administration and otherwise. In fact, the leaders of the Meiji Restoration came from the lower retainer class of this élite and remained at the helm of the new administration for a generation or more. They were the leaders, however; though in absolute number they were negligible. What happened to the bulk of 400,000 *samurai* families? The transition was

[5] See Takejirō Shindō, *Nihon Mengyō Rōdō Ron (Cotton Textile Labour in Japan)*, 1958, p. 356.

not too sudden. The 'status' income in the form of a hereditary stipend, which used to be given in the form of rice, was in 1871 reduced on average to 40 per cent of what it used to be; and commutation was proposed for those prepared to give up a hereditary stipend in return for a lump sum to be used as capital for becoming a farmer or a small producer. Almost one-quarter of the *samurai* families had taken advantage of this commutation measure by 1876; but there still remained 313,000 of them dependent on the 'status' income. Thus the government finally decided in 1876 to carry out a general commutation and distributed transferable government bonds roughly equivalent, at the then purchasing power of *yen*, to the capitalised sum of the annual stipends. Nominally, the status of *samurai* was still retained, but the erstwhile feudal ruling class now became a class of rentier, 83 per cent of them receiving less than 77 *yen* per annum as interest, which was barely sufficient for the minimum standard of living at the time. A year later, in 1877, an inflation began in the wake of the Satsuma rebellion; and during the four years of inflation, which caused a general price rise of about 60 per cent, many of the *samurai* families were forced to sell out their bonds and became pauperised. It was an irony of history that the liquidation of a major portion of the 'status' income was accomplished unwittingly through an inflation which no-one intended and which was a consequence of a local rebellion of the dissatisfied *samurai* class.

The government was aware that in any case a gigantic task of *samurai* rehabilitation was called for, and expended money for land development works for homestead farming by *samurai* families and loaned funds to those who wished to set up small workshops producing all kinds of products. This rehabilitation project was most energetically carried out, particularly after 1882, to cover as many as 180,000 *samurai* families, the largest number for cocoon-raising and silk-reeling (64,757 families), followed by silk and cotton-spinning (56,278) and homestead farming (21,492). But the size of each loan was extremely small, and the creation of a large number of cottage-industry type establishments for a class of people unaccustomed to any enterprise of a commercial character resulted in inefficiency, and many of them fell easy prey to devouring commercial capital or to ubiquitous commission traders. 'Business by *samurai*' (*shizoku no shōhō*) thus became an expression of sarcasm describing any amateurish venture. In 1890, by the time the government closed all the accounts for rehabilitation the law of survival of the fittest had run its course and many of the ex-*samurai* had become irretrievably proletarianised and absorbed into the gamut of a new class relationship.

Before this happened, one must hasten to add, the *samurai* class was in

position to fill the need for able men in government at all levels, as well
in the teaching profession. In 1880, 26,970 out of 36,560 central
overnment staff were ex-*samurai*, and 4295 out of 6658 in the county
ureaucracy and the great majority of the 32,984 town and village
fficers were also from families of the feudal *élite*. In 1882, 32,069 out
85,787 teachers in the public schools also came from this class.[6] In
ddition, as will be shown later, the greater proportion of front-line
ntrepreneurs came from the *samurai* class. Thus it may well be
onceded that, although a major upheaval took place in all aspects of
ociety as a result of the Restoration, the new ruling *élite* was recruited in
e main out of the old ruling class of the feudal society.

Another important group of people who had enjoyed a status of a
nd under feudalism were craftsmen and specialists organised into
uilds. The Restoration government did not wait long before taking
easures to loosen the tie of the guilds. Already in the first year of Meiji,
868, the government issued a special proclamation on 'trading
ractices' and indicated that 'from now on any one will be free to engage
price competition and to increase or decrease the number of members
f his guild'. This was followed in 1872 by a more detailed decree doing
vay with guild restrictions and abolishing the indenture system. There
as not much resistance to this move on the part of guild craftsmen,
ontrary to the case of the guilds in Europe.[7] Their peculiar docility in
apan is probably accounted for, first, by the parasitic character of their
ade, which depended almost entirely on the demand in castle towns for
rticles of feudal warfare and conspicuous consumption and, second, by
e fact that the process of dissolution of the guilds had already been
nder way in the latter part of Tokugawa rule. Moreover, guild
aftsmen were people of some skill and a new pattern of industrial
ructure offered places of employment for many of them. The
djustment required was often the social one of discarding guild security
nd being thrown on to the unpredictable market of 'free' working men.

However, there were different strains among them, each finding its
wn different fate. Firstly, those craftsmen who specialised in making
rmour, swords and peculiarly feudal luxury products were the first to
uffer; and along with them, large numbers of craftsmen in the fields
illed by the competition of cheap imports, such as nail-making, fount it
xtremely difficult to change their trades and were gradually ruined. The
econd category of craftsmen, such as blacksmiths, foundry men,

[6] Mikio Sumiya, op. cit., p. 65
[7] Cf. J. L. and Barbara Hammond, *The Skilled Labourer, 1760–1832* (1919).

carpenters and the like, whose work was closely related to the dail
needs of people in general, could adapt themselves rather more quickl
to the kind of skilled work required in a modern plant or a shipyard, i
not continuing to be independent masters in their old trades. Buildin
trades, in particular, found the transition the smoothest, and probabl
retained the longest semblance of guild-type organisation, with th
hierarchy of master and apprenticeship.

As there were inevitably some trades which declined with the ol
regime, so there emerged new fields of craftsmanship in a new society
such as tailoring, shoe-making, brick-laying and printing. The deman
for them was not easily filled, as can be inferred from the wage-rat
differential[8] which persisted for some time. This group constitutes th
third category of craftsmen into which the astute and the dexterou
moved from all walks of life.

Unfortunately, only scattered statistics are available of the number o
craftsmen that existed in early Meiji years. The statistics of 1882 fo
Yamanashi prefecture, a typically progressive one in those days, show
the structure of gainfully employed among men, as follows:[9]

Total	*127,779*	*100.0 (%*
Agriculture only	85,513	67.0
Craftsmen	9,229	7.2
(of whom, partly in agriculture)	(5,888)	
Manufacturing	7,586	5.9
(of whom, partly in agriculture)	(4,792)	
Commerce, transportation, etc.	25,451	19.9
(of whom, partly in agriculture)	(13,274)	

One is struck by the extent of dependence on land even among men i
other trades, and one suspects that many of the guild craftsmen in bi
cities may have returned before 1882 to their native farmland and hav
carried on their accustomed trade on the side.

In fact, it was quite characteristic of Japan at that time that, while
large amount of disguised unemployment was created in the wake o
Restoration reforms, the forces revealing and isolating it were not stron
enough to destroy the family cohesion which tended to harbour th

---

[8] When the daily wage rate for ordinary craftsmen was 40 to 50 *sen*, tailor
commanded as much as 70 *sen* per day.

[9] Complied from Tokei-In, *Kainokuni Genzai, Jinbetsu Shirabe (Survey o
Residents of the Province of Kai)*, as reproduced in Mikio Sumiya, op. cit., p. 49

nfortunate under its wing. This accounts, in a large measure, for the
fficulty encountered in recruiting the unskilled workers that were
eded in large numbers in mines, for railway building and other
onstruction works of the social overhead type.

Mines of all kinds had existed before the Restoration; but the scale of
ining activities expanded tremendously after it, and the demand for
iners leapt up, with the supply constantly lagging. A solution was
ught in the use of prisoners. The Miike coalmine, for example, started
sing them in 1875 and expanded their number to 2000 by 1882. The
Iiike's example was soon followed by the Horonai mine and others.
he government condoned this on the pretext that prisoners could learn
omething useful. But it was in the end the management which found the
se of prisoners not only rather intractable but also detrimental to the
orale of co-working non-prisoners, and the practice was terminated in
ost places by 1894. In their place came vagrants and fugitive criminals
nd the situation was little improved until Korean immigrants came
uch later.

The use of prisoners was not confined only to mining. Records show
at they were enlisted in reclamation work for the Yokohama shipyard
nd also for railway construction at a number of places. Needless to say,
owever, they constituted a small minority among the scores of
ousands of unskilled common labourers who were required at the
me. In isolated instances it was possible to mobilise seasonally idle
easantry for local construction works, but in general a much more
stematic form of recruitment was needed. This was particularly true of
ilway construction which, with the modest beginning of the 18-mile
ne between Tokyo and Yokohama in 1872, expanded rapidly all over
e country, to achieve a length of 300 miles by 1886 and 2000 miles by
893. It is estimated, for example, that in 1892 there were upwards of
0,000 road workers continually engaged in railway construction. This
as a type of common labour which often had to move from one place to
nother, requiring a peculiar type of discipline quite different from that
f factory labour. To meet this need, a contracting system developed
hereby the head contractor acted like a captain of his private army,
ith appropriate levels of lieutenants between him and the horde of
rivates recruited off and on under the contractor's own responsibility.

SKILLED WORKERS AND TRAINING PROGRAMMES

here were skills in Japan before the Restoration which were relevant to
e arts encouraged by the feudal mode of life. But the types of skill

required in the modernisation process were of the kind related
mechanical arts in such industries as steel-making, engineering, railw
telephone and telegraph and surveying, and Japan was only at
threshold of learning these skills when the new regime came ii
existence. The government was aware of this lacuna, and when they
up the Department of Industry (*Kōbushō*) in 1870, its frame of referei
included the establishment of an institution for training engineers. Tl
a Technical School (*Kōgakuryō*) was inaugurated in August 1871, w
the senior teaching staff consisting almost entirely of foreigners. On
list of this staff there were 41 British, 7 Italians and 1 French, headed
Henry Dyer and William E. Ayrton. Very high salaries were paid
them: Dyer, for example, then only 25 years-old, received 600 *yen*
month, which exceeded by 100 *yen* the salary of a Cabinet Minister.
most intensive curriculum was planned for the students (eleven and
half hours of classroom work every day) who went through a two-yε
preparatory course, followed by two years each of specialised educati
and practical training. The six divisions of the Technical Sch
consisted of civil engineering, mechanical engineering, electrical co
munications, architecture, applied chemistry and metallurgy, and mi
engineering. Although it was discontinued in 1885, it produced in
short life more than 200 engineers of first-rate calibre, each of whom
his own way performed a pioneering function in the spreading
western techniques.[10]

These newly trained engineers were to be placed at the top of t
pyramid of technical personnel required for the modern engineeri
industry. The bottom of the pyramid was to consist of an incomparal
larger number of trained-on-the-job skilled workers, qualified to hanε
directly specific machines and tools and, if necessary, to repair the
Whence were they to come?

They, too, had to be trained from scratch, although there is no dοι
that some of the craftsmen in the Tokugawa society, accustomed
handling metals, already had enough adaptability to perform some
the new tasks which came into being. The earliest and most effecti
places of practical training were the government factories, which at t
time were mainly concentrated in the armaments and shipbuildi
fields. In fact, the modern metals and engineering factories were almε
entirely in public hands at the start; and even after the across-the-boa

[10] For the details on curriculum, regulations, names of teachers with th
salaries, names of graduating students, etc., see *Kōbushō Enkaku Hōkoku
Report on the History of the Department of Industry)* reproduced in *Meiji Zει
Zaisei Keizai Shiryō Shūsei*, vol. 17, especially pp. 343–411.

transfer of government factories to private hands in the period after 1880, the metals and engineering industries remained armament-oriented and under government ownership for some time.

Considering this background, it appears only natural that the training of skilled workmen in the metals and engineering industries was almost entirely in the hands of the government. So far as the hiring of foreign technical specialists was concerned, it antedated the Restoration by a number of years, in as much as the Bakufu government had already been intent on introducing western arts in the military sphere. Thus Hardes, a Dutch naval engineer, came to Japan in 1857 and supervised the construction of the Nagasaki Iron Works which later grew into the Nagasaki Shipyard (or Mitsubishi Shipyard). Again, François Léon Verny, a French naval engineer, was invited in 1866 to assist in building the Yokosuka Iron Works, which in 1871 became the Yokosuka Shipyard, a government plant. Verny, in particular, remained, with thirty-one other French technicians, even after the Restoration, and assumed the task of training skilled workers in shipbuilding until 1877. A standard work on the history of modern shipbuilding in Japan records that 'several thousand able skilled workers were produced'[11] before the French advisers left the country. It is also noteworthy that shipbuilding spearheaded the development of modern industries in Japan, outstripping in relative terms the development of such basic industries as steel and machine tools.

However, on-the-job training under the guidance of foreign experts was essentially an operation of limited scope. Thus the government decided in 1872 to open two schools, both attached to Yokosuka Shipyard, one for the training of more advanced technicians at foreman level and the other for the training of skilled workers. These two schools, for the moment, apparently satisfied the needs, which remained somewhat limited so far as the metals and engineering industries were concerned. But a broader need was soon felt, and the government decided in 1881 to establish, under the jurisdiction of the Ministry of Education, the Tokyo School for Skilled Workers, with the intention of providing similar schools in other prefectures. Education and training at these schools, however, turned out to be too advanced, in the sense that the graduating students felt encouraged to seek positions higher than that of a foreman. Thus the government sought to set up schools for the practical training of less ambitious youths and experimented after 1886 with an 'apprentice training centre', attached to the Tokyo School of

---

[11] *Nihon Kinsei Zōsen Shi (History of Modern Shipbuilding in Japan)* p. 934.

Commerce. But this, too, had only a lukewarm success. In the end it turned out that men who had come into armament factories or government model plants as ordinary workers became skilled through practice over the years and later moved on to various private plants as the leading personnel in the corps of skilled workmen. Private firms in the modern industries, which in general only became viable later, adopted the practice of training men to different levels of skill in their own shops, and for that reason, they considered their men to be their own 'property', as it were, and found the system of seniority and permanent employeeship more congenial to their employment practice.

4 EDUCATION IN GENERAL

Arinori Mori, one of the early Meiji leaders whose contribution in the field of education was especially outstanding, spoke at the Saitama Normal School in 1885, shortly before he assumed the post of Minister of Education, as follows: 'Our country must move from its third-class position to second-class, and from second-class to first; and ultimately to the leading position among all countries of the world. The best way to do this is by laying the foundations of elementary education'.

There is little doubt that the qualifications the Meiji leaders held in view as characterising a 'first-class' country were a 'prosperous economy and strong military' (*fukoku kyōhei*) and that there was full awareness of the relevance of education to economic development. In fact, the same Arinori Mori, while stationed at Washington as Japan's first diplomatic representative to the United States in 1872, addressed, on his own initiative, a letter to a group of prominent Americans seeking 'advice and information' on 'the educational affairs of Japan' and wrote: 'The particular points to which I invite your attention are as follows: The effect of education (1) upon the material prosperity of a country; (2) upon its commerce; (3) upon its agricultural and industrial interests; (4) upon the social, moral, and physical conditions of the people; and (5) its influence upon the laws and government'.[12] It is noteworthy that the first three of the five points listed were exclusively concerned with economic matters. Mori's letter was answered by thirteen Americans, including Charles W. Eliot of Harvard, Theodore D. Woolsey of Yale, and William A. Stearns of Amherst; and their replies acted as seeds, as it were, in the near virgin soil of educational opportunities in Japan. One of the thirteen, David Murray of Rutgers University, who had written

[12] Arinori Mori, *Education in Japan* (New York, 1873).

an essay-long reply, was invited in 1873 to come to Japan as 'Superintendent of Educational Affairs in the Empire of Japan and Adviser to the Japanese Imperial Minister of Education', receiving a monthly salary of 600 *yen*, the same as that of the Prime Minister. For almost six years until January 1879, when he left Japan, Murray was a guiding spirit in the pioneering work of laying foundations for the universal education which made rapid progress, largely after his departure. The following paragraph out of his original response to Mori's inquiry was especially remembered and repeated by the Meiji leaders:

> Japan, in respect to the Asiatic continent and the western coast of America, holds a position almost identical to that of England in respect to the European continent and the eastern coast of America. It requires but the introduction of the modern appliances of commerce and the judicious encouragement of the Government, to create out of Japan an equally colossal commercial power. It is, however, the work of time, and in that work education must be a principal instrument.[13]

Setting the role of education thus firmly on a practical basis as 'a principal instrument' for making Japan a leading commercial power, the Meiji leaders emphasised time and again the importance of drawing out their potentialities from everyone. Yukichi Fukuzawa's *Encouragement of Learning*, published in 1872, with a resounding opening sentence: 'Heaven did not create men above men nor put men under men, it is said', represented most eloquently the spirit of the time. And the Preamble to the Fundamental Code of Education, 1872, spelled out the liberal view then held on education, which while showing, on the one hand, the government determination that 'there shall, in the future, be no community with an illiterate family, nor a family with an illiterate person' exhorted the nation, on the other, to assume its own responsibility at grassroots level for the education of its young. The concluding paragraph of the Preamble said:

> Heretofore . . . the evil tradition which looked upon learning as the privilege of the *samurai* and his superiors, and as being for the state, caused many to depend upon the government for the expenses of education, even for such items as food and clothing; and, failing to receive such support, many wasted their lives by not going to school.

[13] Quoted in Herbert Passin, *Society and Education in Japan* (1965), p. 219.

Hereafter such errors must be corrected, and every man shall, of his own accord, subordinate all other matter to the education of his children.[14]

It is remarkable that the awareness of the need for energetic guidance from the centre was combined, in the minds of the Meiji leaders, with the insight that success depended on voluntary enthusiasm on the part of the masses of the people. The policy followed was in this dialectic spirit; and although the central government expended a great deal of money on the hiring of foreign teachers for advanced schools and the sending of Japanese students abroad, they pursued the policy of making local governments share a greater part of the cost of education and of acquiescing in a tuition charge of 25 to 50 *sen* per month for what was intended to be compulsory elementary education. It was not until 1900 that elementary education became nominally free in all parts of the country.

Thus, in spite of the exhortation from the centre, based upon a keen awareness of the importance of general education for national development, progress in the spread of elementary education was somewhat slow, as can be seen from the following statistics of percentages of schoolchildren compulsorily enrolled:[15]

	Male and Female (%)	*Male* (%)	*Female* (%)
1873	28.1	39.9	15.1
1880	41.1	58.7	21.9
1890	48.9	65.1	31.1
1900	81.5	90.6	71.7
1910	98.1	98.8	97.4

Modern school construction also lagged badly, as an 1875 survey shows that only 18 per cent of the schools were housed in new buildings, 40 per cent in Buddhist temples, 33 per cent in private homes, and the rest in public buildings of sundry kinds.[16] The situation as regards the

[14] Quoted in Kumaji Yoshida, 'European and American Influences in Japanese Education', in Inazo Nitobe *et al., Western Influences in Modern Japan* (1931), p. 35.
[15] Ministry of Education, *Japan's Growth and Education*, p. 160.
[16] Tomitaro Karasawa, *Nihon no Kyōiku Shi (History of Japanese Education)* (1962), p. 219.

supply of teachers was actually worse, in as much as it took longer to train a teacher than to put up a school-building and the pay scale for teachers was for a long time less than adequate. By 1876, for example, only one-sixth of the 52,000 teachers had been trained in the new normal schools;[17] and the supporting document for the Revised Educational Ordinance of 1880 was even more pessimistic, saying that 'only one out of every 10 teachers in the country has graduated from Normal School. They know nothing about the techniques of teaching'.[18] Nevertheless, for the *samurai*, particularly in the provinces, teaching had a special appeal, less as a profession than as a 'heavenly calling', and the supply somehow kept up with the demand.

All in all, the spread of education was not an easy task, what with the self-imposed constraints in the earlier period and the pressing demand by industries for the young irrespective of their training. One may say, however, that the early emphasis on the *élite* training paid well, and that by the time the scope of modernisation widened to require a broader base of the labour force with a minimum education, the universal schooling had its tortuous preparatory stage behind it and was in a position to cope with the demands of the day. In this process, one should probably not fail to mention the advantage which the Japanese have had in having a common language for the nation as a whole and one which could be adapted for modern scientific usage. Although there is no denying the fact that deliberate efforts were made by many to simplify the language and to coin a thousand and one modern scientific terms, it is also true that the language was highly malleable, with phonetics of its own combined with Chinese characters, and that any of the scientific disciplines could be taught at the most elementary level in the vernacular. For a latecomer like Japan in modern industrial civilisation the advantage of this happy state of affairs can certainly not be overemphasised.

5 WHENCE THE ENTREPRENEURS?

Japan developed essentially on a basis of capitalism. This means that the driving force of the economy was in the person of the private, risk-taking entrepreneur. To the extent that the state often took the initiative in starting a new industry, one might say that the original risk was taken by the state, and there developed, in actual fact, a peculiar category of

[17] Mombushō, *Gakusei 50-nen Shi (Fifty Years of the School System)* (1954), p. 46.

[18] Quoted in Herbert Passin, op. cit., p. 75.

entrepreneurs, called 'seishō' or businessmen with political affiliation, who thrived by taking advantage of the state's intervention in business. Even in this case, however, entrepreneurs were essentially risk-taking, in the sense that for them the fact of political rivalry between politicians constituted a datum for the business calculation for which they themselves were ultimately responsible. Therefore it is still worth asking: whence the entrepreneurs?

The feudal period which preceded the Restoration was characterised, as was mentioned earlier, by the differentiation of hereditary status, classified into (i) *samurai*, (ii) farmers, (iii) craftsmen, and (iv) merchants. Towards the end of the Tokugawa rule, a large part of the *samurai* class became impoverished and fell into heavy indebtedness to the merchant class. The latter as a whole became economically more and more powerful. But, significantly enough, the prosperous merchant class did not easily break from its convention of subservience to the *samurai*, and thus also to the new ruling class of the Restoration. The task of path-breaking entrepreneurship was not congenial to them, and on the whole they followed, rather than led, the modernisation process in the economic sphere. If some of them, like the firm of Mitsui, succeeded in carrying out a pioneering task, it was because the hereditary head of the firm was wise enough to bring able ex-*samurai* into the position of general manager.

Probably no one better typified the versatile, enlightened, forward-looking entrepreneurs of the Meiji period than Eiichi Shibusawa (1840–1931) who was born of a farmer's family, turned civil servant under the Restoration government and left it after five years to devote the rest of his long life to the promotion of modern industries in the private sector. There were two guiding principles which he held firmly and put into practice. One was the advantage of the corporate form of business enterprise and the other was the breaking down of the preponderance of official power. To his colleagues who tried to dissuade him from resigning an official post in 1873, Shibusawa is said to have replied:

The foundation of a country is in commerce and industry. We can afford to have mediocre civil servants, but men in commerce have to be capable and wise . . . In the past, our nation held the *samurai* class in esteem; and now they consider it a matter of higher honour to become bureaucrats while feeling ashamed of being engaged in commerce. This is like putting the cart before the horse. The most urgent task facing our country today is to sweep away this fallacious view, to raise the social position of men in commerce, to enlist men of talent into such endeavour and to promote them into a class of people viewed as the model of virtues among the people.[19]

Shibusawa was 33 years-old at that time; and from then on, until he retired from active work at the age of 77, he would not accept, despite repeated entreaties, a single governmental post, including that of the governorship of the Bank of Japan. Instead, starting with the presidency of the First National Bank in 1873, Shibusawa lent his able hand to the creation of almost every one of the modern industries of Japan, such as paper-manufacturing (1873), insurance (1878), private railways (1881), coastal shipping (1882), modern large-scale cotton-spinning (1883), chemical fertilisers (1887) and beer-brewing (1888), to name only a few in the earlier years. Altogether, he was associated, in one capacity or another, with more than 500 companies; and it was characteristic of him consistently to shun personal enrichment and meticulously to avoid political affiliations. To write Shibusawa's biography would be tantamount to chronicling almost the entire history of the rise of modern industries in Japan. In fact, his interest went far beyond the realm of business, and he is counted, for example, as a co-founder of the Training Centre of Commercial Practices which later grew into the Tokyo Higher School of Commerce, now Hitsotsubashi University – an institution always considered to be the training ground for 'captains of industry' in the private sector in contrast to Tokyo University which was regarded as the nursery of bureaucracy.

Few would disagree that a list of the most prominent pioneers in business in the first half of the Meiji Era (roughly to the end of the nineteenth century) should include, along with Shibusawa, such names as:

Tomoatsu Godai (1835–85), who contributed more than anyone else to making Osaka the centre of trade and industry, himself engaged above all in mining;
Yatarō Iwasaki (1834–85), who founded the famed Mitsubishi multi-industry structure, with its earlier success in shipping;
Rizaemon Minomura (1821–77) and Takashi Masuda (1847–1938), each of whom as general manager of the Mitsui firm succeeded in keeping that ancient conservative merchant house in the front line of modernisation; and

[19] Quoted in Takao Tsuchiya, *Nihon Shihonshugi no Keieishiteki Kenkyu (A Study of Japanese Capitalism as Business History)* (1954), p. 92.

Saihei Hirose (1828–1914), who helped to transform the old Sumitomo copper-trading firm into a modern multi-industry firm.

It is significant that none of these was from the merchant class, Iwasaki being a so-called 'country *samurai*', Hirose the son of a doctor, and the other three having come from *samurai* families.

Shibusawa was exceptionally correct in his association with political leaders. But most of the business leaders at the top were in a greater or lesser degree of the type who climbed the ladder of success by clever steering of their political counterparts, and a number of them, as is well known, consolidated themselves later into the uniquely Japanese monopoly structures called *zaibatsu*. This form of organisation, having tentacles extended into a variety of business pursuits, was able to distribute risks, and having close inside affiliation with political leaders, was able to internalise all kinds of external economies, and the economy of Japan grew and prospered with the rise of *zaibatsu* during the subsequent period. At this time, the wisdom of *zaibatsu* leadership lay in the recruiting of fresh blood of vigorous entrepreneurship whatever its family origin might be.

IV GENERAL CONCLUSIONS

The tasks of modern economic development require all kinds of men. Even in a society which is centrally planned, a system of rewards has to be devised in such a way that human resources with differing abilities and qualifications can be allocated in the economically most efficient manner. Rewards consist essentially of monetary returns and/or personal satisfactions based upon social esteem or a sense of fulfilment. What can we say of the system of rewards in Meiji Japan, which undoubtedly had something to do with the allocation of human resources which actually took place?

What drives one to seek a certain job is above all the necessity for living, and then the differential in monetary rewards or the non-monetary satisfaction one gets from a certain line of endeavour. One may say that the Meiji Japan combined all of these most successfully. Aside from the reward for the entrepreneur class, which must have been satisfying beyond its monetary equivalent, the Meiji society developed a set of values oriented towards Emperor worship and service to the nation. Consequently, the monetary reward was not everything. This was a situation which made it easier to recruit men of talent into such a profession as teaching and to pay far higher salaries to foreigners than to Japanese. At the other extreme, the heavy land tax and the exorbitant rent in kind kept the cultivating peasantry in a condition no better than under the feudal period and caused the supply price of common labour and female factory hands to be controlled by the bare necessity of living.

It would be an interesting exercise in comparative research to attempt a calculation of the relative dispersion among pay scales of different professions in the economy, all of them in relation to the per capita income at the time. This last figure has to be a rough estimate in as much as Japan's historical statistics are not adequate. But there is one figure that is of ubiquitous relevance and of tolerable accuracy, the price of rice, one *koku* (150 kilograms) of which used to be considered in those days as a unit of basic need for staples for a year and one *shō* (1.5 kilograms) of which was regarded as the minimum daily wage for the commonest labour. Now the decade average cost of rice per *koku* in Tokyo at wholesale prices rose from 6.36 *yen* during 1868–77 to 7.40 *yen* for 1878–87, to 8.08 *yen* for 1888–97, and to 13.33 *yen* for 1898–1907. In view of the fact that the retail price was generally one-third higher than this, one may say that one *shō* of polished rice cost 8.5 *sen* in the first decade of the Meiji era and rose to 17.8 *sen* in the fourth. Table 4.3 compares various wage and pay scales in the early Meiji years with such an average price of rice in the second decade (1878–87) and reveals a clear picture of extreme spread. Whereas female factory hands in silk-reeling or cotton-spinning mills generally received less than the equivalent of one *shō* of rice per day, teachers received four to ten times as much, skilled workers nine times, fresh graduates from Tokyo University more than fourteen times, and the highest civil servant, that is a Vice Minister, a hundred times more. It is likely that per capita income in Japan in those days was fairly close to the value of one *shō* of rice.[20] Therefore, if we expressed the multiples against the per capita income, the resulting picture of relative income spread among employed persons would turn out to be little different from the one revealed in Table 4.3.

Such a wide spread in the pay scale between employed persons is in striking contrast to present-day Japan. The annual per capita income (national income at market prices divided by the number of population)

[20] *Kōgyō Iken (Memorandum on Promotion of Industries)* (1883), edited by Masana Mayeda, estimated that the per capita cost of living for the 'well-to-do' was 110 *yen* per annum, that for 'medium standard' 60 *yen* and that for 'the lowest' 20 *yen*. The weighted average for the nation as a whole comes out at 43 *yen*. If we divide this by 365, we obtain the per capita daily living expenditure of 11.6 *sen* for 1883.

TABLE 4.3   WAGE AND PAY SCALE IN RELATION TO PRICE OF
RICE, EARLY MEIJI YEARS

	sen	Years applicable	Relatives (Rice price = 100)
Price of rice, 1 *shō*	9.5	(1878–87)	100
Daily wage			
Silk-reeling, female	5–15	(1880s)	53–158
Cotton-spinning, male	17.1	(1889)	180
Cotton-spinning, female	8.2	(1889)	86
Skilled worker	90	(1883)	948
Carpenter	50	(1879)	526
Stonemason	70	(1879)	737
Monthly pay ÷ 30			
Teachers	40–100	(1876)	412–1052
New graduates from Tokyo University	133–166	(1887)	1400–1747
Non-commissioned civil servants (average)	70.6	(1878)	743
Commissioned government officials	110–972	(1890)	1,158–10,232
Cabinet minister	1390	(1890)	14,632

Source: The price of rice was estimated by multiplying the Fukagawa wholesale price quotation by 1.3. Daily-wage figures have been given earlier in the text. Monthly-pay figures are based on the information supplied in H. Passin, op. cit., p. 75, for teachers, Imperial Decree No. 37, 23 July 1887 for new Tokyo University graduates, and *Meiji Bunka Zenshū*, Vol. 10, pp. 505–6, 531 for others.

TABLE 4.4   CASH EARNINGS INCLUDING BONUS PAYMENTS, 1978

Blue-collar male workers, aged 18 to 19, in establishments employing 10 to 99	80
Blue-collar male workers, aged 50 to 54, in establishments employing 1000 or more	245
Heads of divisions (college graduates), aged 50 to 54, in business establishments employing 1000 or more	566
Annual payments for members of Diet (national parliament)	903
Salaries received by executives in average-size corporations	1332

Source: The Ministry of Labour, *Chingin Kōzō Kihon Tōkei Chōsa (Basic Statistical Research on Wage Structure)*.

in 1978 was 1,501,900 *yen* (or $7500 at the year-average exchange rate in that year); against this, cash earnings of regularly employed workers in all the industries averaged 2,824,536 *yen* (1.88 times), and Table 4.4 gives relative differentials for some typical categories of gainfully employed persons for the year 1978 as percentages to the annual per capita income.

It is most likely that in the early Meiji years, when the mobilisation of able men into important posts of all kinds was essential, it was necessary, in spite of the spiritual and honorific elements that were inculcated as a matter of national policy, to attract men by high remuneration. As time went on, the spread in pay scales was rapidly narrowed, usually by raising the bottom scale while keeping the top unchanged.[21] In addition, a progressive income tax was instituted in Japan in 1887 and various social security measures subsequently came to be introduced to bring about income redistribution effect through public finance, and the degree of income equality which now prevails, at least among employed persons, appears to be socially accepted as normal. It may well be that the course of economic development makes it possible for a country to narrow the spread of remuneration required for sifting human resources among different levels of qualified positions.

[21] This trend continued in the most recent period as shown by the declining spread between the starting salary (regular cash earnings not including bonus payments) for new recruits and that for those aged 50 to 59 who have worked for thirty years or more in the same establishment (establishments employing 1000 or more). For blue-collar workers, the relative stood at 638 in 1961 and steadily declined to 313 in 1978, and for white-collar workers, the relative stood at 579 in 1961 and also steadily declined to 294 in 1978 (source: as for Table 4.4).

Comments on Professor Tsuru's Paper: 'Economic Development and Human Resources: Japan's Experience'

H. M. A. Onitiri

Nigeria

As the major world economies become increasingly concerned with the pressure of Japanese competition, developing countries continue to search eagerly through the history books to find out just how a country with such obvious geographical disadvantages, most especially the lack of basic raw materials, has achieved such an impressive and spectacular economic growth, and attained such a high level of productivity, over a comparatively short period of history.

This is why the economic history of Japan has become a major reference for development planners in the developing countries. Indeed, so much has been written about Japan's economic growth that one sometimes wonders whether there is anything more that could be said on the subject. However, like many other examples of remarkable and rapid development, the factors involved are so complex and the relevant economic and non-economic factors are so intertwined that a new look at the subject often provides fresh insights.

Professor Tsuru has taken another peep into one period of Japan's spectacular economic history and drawn our attention to several critical factors that need to be taken into account in understanding and explaining the process of Japanese economic growth during this period. He has focused attention in particular on the role played by the development of human resources at all levels. In a brief paper, Professor Tsuru could not touch on all the crucial factors. However, his emphasis on the role of the development of human resources is very well taken. For a country suffering from a shortage of basic raw materials, the major explanation for rapid economic development must be found in the ability to add value to resources imported from the outside world. But other factors are no less important, such as the peculiar relationship between Japanese governments and private enterprise and the unique relationship that has always prevailed between Japanese employers and their workers, which largely explains the comparative stability of industrial relations.

In a situation in which economic and social factors are so inextricably intertwined, it is never easy to draw comparisons and examples that can be of value in other societies. However, the lessons of Japanese economic development should not be lost upon present-day developing countries. First, if a country with a slender raw material base can achieve such spectacular progress within a comparatively short period, those deeloping countries that possess an abundance of raw materials should egin to ask themselves why, in spite of their favourable endowment of atural resources, they remain poor, some of them so poor as to be capable of providing even the most elementary means of sustenance r their populations.

Secondly, few cases in recent economic history show the importance f technology in economic development more than the Japanese xperience. It provides ample illustration of the great advantages ajoyed in the world today by those who possess the technology and xpertise to exploit raw materials and fashion them into high-value-dded products, in contrast to the hopeless situation of those who ossess abundant raw materials, but lack the technology and the xpertise to exploit them by themselves, and to process them beyond inimal beneficiation, which adds little to producers' incomes but nsiderably reduces the cost of transportation to importers in de-eloped countries, who are the real beneficiaries of the ultimate value dded.

Thirdly, the Japanese experience underlines the need of raw material roducers for more equitable international arrangements for the narketing and processing of raw materials, that will enable poor eveloping countries to retain for the benefit of their population an ncreasing share of the value added to their raw material exports.

How can developing countries profit from the Japanese experience? his question must be answered, of course, with a good deal of rcumspection, since the widely different social situations do not allow r a simple transfer of the Japanese experience to the developing ountries. But even with this caution, there are at least three areas, lentified in Professor Tsuru's paper, where Japanese experience can rovide some useful lessons for developing countries. For one thing, the apanese experience should lead developing countries to keep constant atch over the benefits they are getting from the exploitation and xportation of their raw materials. There are too many cases where aluable raw materials are exploited and exported with very little value the producing countries. For example, a considerable part of the huge orests of tropical Africa has been exploited with little control and xported in the form of logs with little value added, and the fear has now een expressed that within a very short time Africa's valuable forests will ave disappeared, with serious consequences for future development. gain, how does one explain the exportation of valuable metals, such as opper, for many years at world prices below the costs of production, at time when dire predictions are being made about future world shortages? The case for world stabilisation of primary commodity price has never been so obvious, and yet the response of the develope countries has been anything but enthusiastic.

A second lesson to be learnt from Japan is the advantage of a clos working relationship between government and private enterprise. Thes days, this issue has become so mixed up with the ideological conflic between the great powers that many developing countries, buffeted b pressures from East and West, have not been able to focus on thos domestic institutional arrangements that are best suited to their ow particular circumstances. On the one hand, attempts by governments t control the major sectors of economic activity, without adequat administrative and management capability, have led to widesprea inefficiency and waste, while on the other, wholesale reliance on th private sector has merely placed vital sectors of the economy in th hands of powerful foreign enterprises. True, the Japanese experienc illustrates the possibility of having a framework in which privat enterprises are allowed a great deal of independence and initiative whil still subject to substantial governmental control and guidance. But it ha to be remembered that Japanese enterprises have always been controlle and managed by Japanese personnel, with foreign expertise playing rather marginal role. The situation is the exact opposite in man developing countries, and the motivation for extensive governmen control often arises from the need to reduce foreign domination of th national economy.

A third lesson that can be drawn from the Japanese experience is th importance of moderating the growth of money incomes while main taining a high level of productivity. In the developing countries, th tendency is for money incomes to grow rapidly in the face of stagnan productivity. The peculiar relationship which prevails between Japanes employers and their workers, and which has contributed to industria harmony and high levels of productivity, is, of course, rooted i Japanese culture and cannot easily be replicated elsewhere. To attain th same degree of industrial harmony in the developing countries woul require a comprehensive approach to incomes policy and a reorientatio of development planning to promote more equitable income distri bution. Furthermore, the exploitation of labour, particularly that o women and children, which played some role in the early years o Japanese economic growth, is now both politically impracticable an socially unacceptable. For example, rural producers of food an agricultural raw materials are no longer prepared to toil and sweat t feed the population and factories in the growing urban concentration while they themselves enjoy few of the benefits associated with modern economic and social development. Rather, they vote with their feet to join the vast army of the unemployed in urban centres, with consequent decline in food production. Furthermore, such is the strength of organised labour in the urban centres that the presence of a large unemployed labour force has rarely mitigated the tendency for wages to rise faster than productivity.

Low productivity and higher costs in turn slow down the spread of education and other essential services to the vast majority of the population. Added to all this, is the situation created by the rising cost of imported inputs, most especially of energy.

Entangled in so many vicious circles, it is not surprising that only few countries, even among those with abundant supplies of raw materials, have been able to establish the basic conditions for self-sustaining and self-reliant development. Complex as the situation is in many developing countries today, an approach to development that focuses on the rapid development of human resources and that aims at improving the productivity of resources devoted to this vital sector, would provide a motive force for rapid economic and social development. But it needs to be emphasised that the success of this approach will depend on firm policies in many other areas. The key role of human development and the wider context within which it needs to be considered are very well expressed in the conclusion to the World Development Report, 1980.[1] It says:

Nothing can make widespread absolute poverty melt away overnight. And human development at best can do only part of the job. Without effective policies on other fronts, and without active and enlightened support from the rest of the world, progress will be agonizingly slow. But these other policies will not be sufficient. The most valuable resource any country has is its people, the means and the end of economic advance.

If considered within this wider context and in the light of the new internal and external conditions that developing countries have to cope with, the Japanese experience can provide useful lessons for development policies.

---

[1] Published by the International Bank for Reconstruction and Development.

**Comments on Professor Tsuru's Paper: 'Economic Development an
Human Resources: Japan's Experience'**
Bruno Contini
Italy

Professor Tsuru has pointed out in a fascinating paper a number o
crucial aspects of the role of human resources in the history of Japan'
development. Let me recall the following three:

   (i) the role of education (by the beginning of the century Japan'
       primary school enrolment was as high as that of most Europea
       countries as well as that of the United States);
  (ii) the role of women's participation in factory work in the earl
       stages of the industrialisation process of Japan;
 (iii) the role of the political system, in particular: (a) how it affecte
       the break-up of the privileges of the old bourgeoisie, the warric
       and landowner's class (the *samurai* and the guilds); (b) how
       then managed to utilise the same system of cultural values t
       enhance new patterns of entrepreneurship.

There is, it seems to me, a lot to be learned from Professor Tsuru
account of the Japanese experience when looking at some of the majo
problems that the developing world is facing today. What I fin
particularly appealing is the renewed suggestion that economic facto
alone cannot lead to development unless coupled with a political syste
capable of dealing with change within a framework of appropriat
cultural values.

Needless to say, cultural values point in many different directions: on
which has been extremely important since the early days of industriali
ation is the attitude towards women's work. It is remarkable, if n
surprising, that in all the less developed countries that have had a recor
of rapid growth of GNP and exports in the last twenty years or so, th
participation rate of women has without exception increased ver
substantially in the same period. On the other hand, it is also true that i
all the LDCs in which the participation rate of women has remaine
unchanged or has evolved slowly, patterns of only sluggish growth hav
been observed.

I would like, however, to draw your attention to another empirica
finding that has puzzled me for some years, and that seems strongly t
confirm the suggestion that a much better understanding of the workin
of the socio-political system is necessary in the field of developmer
economics. I have looked at a cross-section of thirty-one countries (non

TABLE 4C.1   EMPLOYMENT AND AVERAGE PRODUCT IN THE
TERTIARY SECTORS
(employment or product in manufacturing = 100)

	Employment	Average product
I. Industrialised 'Welfare States'		
Sweden (1967)	114	119
Netherlands (1970)	127	91
Norway (1967)	135	105
Finland (1967)	112	104
UK	110	102
II. Other industrialised countries		
Belgium (1967)	117	110
Austria (1967)	103	78
W. Germany (1970)	90	98
France (1970)	117	66
USA (1970)	188[a]	89
Canada (1970)	184[a]	97
Japan (1970)	137[a]	80
III. Less developed countries		
Brazil (1973)	204	148
Chile (1976)	181	117
Mexico (1973)	151	121
Venezuela (1974)	208	105
India (1973)	143	120
Iran (1973)	96	205
Israel (1973)	172	100
S. Korea (1974)	115	120
Malaysia (1974)	254	72
Pakistan (1973)	144	144
Philippines (1974)	142	158
Singapore (1974)	150	129
Turkey (1974)	197	111
Taiwan (1969)	181	131
Lebanon (1972)	220	157
Syria (1972)	147	148
Egypt (1972)	188	121
Morocco (1972)	172	150
Tunisia (1972)	197	134

[a] Manufacturing services are included in the tertiary sectors. In all other countries they are instead classified as manufacturing.

Source United Nations, *National Accounts*; International Labour Office, *Work and Employment Statistics*; OECD, *National Accounts and Labour Statistics*.

belonging to the Socialist bloc) that can be fairly neatly grouped in three exclusive subsets (Table 4C.1): (i) the industrialised welfare states of the western world (five countries: Sweden, Norway, Finland, Netherlands, United Kingdom); (ii) a group of highly industrialised countries of the western world (seven countries: Belgium, Austria, West Germany, France, United States of America, Canada, Japan); (iii) a group of nineteen scattered LDCs, including all the largest ones.

Consider the following four indicators: employment in manufacturing; employment in tertiary sectors (that is the trades, the services, banking and insurance institutions and the government sector); average product in manufacturing; average product in tertiary sectors. A rather distinct pattern emerges:

(1) In the countries of the first group of so-called welfare states employment in the tertiary sectors is about 10–35 per cent higher than in manufacturing and average product in the tertiary sectors is higher than in manufacturing.

(2) In the second group of highly industrialised countries, employment in the tertiary sectors is also somewhat higher than in manufacturing, but average product is lower than in manufacturing.

(3) In all but one of the less developed countries belonging to the third group, employment in the tertiary sectors is at least 40 per cent higher than in manufacturing (sometimes more than twice as high); in all but one, average product in the tertiary is substantially higher than in manufacturing.

As a first rough approximation, let average product be an estimate of average income earned in each sector: the assumption is probably a better one in the LDCs, where productive units are small, often family-run enterprises. Economic theory suggests that income differentials between sectors reflect productivity differentials. Apparently the differences between the first two groups of industrialised countries fit the conventional economic framework; however, if we turn to the third group of LDCs, the same explanation cannot possibly hold: it is in fact very hard to believe that average productivity in the tertiary sectors of these countries can be so much higher than that of the manufacturing sector, as the figures reported in Table 4C.1 imply according to the theory (considering also that recorded employment in the tertiary is so much higher as well). The answer must lie somewhere else. I have been tempted by the following explanation which might appeal more to a political scientist than an economist: in many of the countries which have yet to reach a consolidated industrial structure, the role of ensuring social equilibrium and political consensus is usually entrusted to the national bourgeoisie, which operates mainly in the private tertiary sectors (trades, tourism, services) and in the public sector. The pay-off for the social strata who perform in this role is guaranteed by the existence of solid protective devices, administrative barriers to entry aimed at preventing competition, ample possibilities of tax evasion. The proposition that I would like to bring to your attention is that these are mechanisms that allow vast redistributive movements from manufacturing (and possibly agriculture) towards the tertiary sectors, and that these mechanisms are the result of deliberate strategies aimed at the consolidation of the status quo.

As I was listening this morning to Professor Prebisch's paper, and Jagdish Bhagwati's discussion of it, I realised that there are some interesting similarities between his framework and my own: his 'privileged consumption society' roughly coincides with what I have called privileged social strata that operate in the tertiary sectors. Bhagwati objected to this terminology by pointing out that the savings ratio of the upper-income classes is often found to be higher than Prebisch's analysis (and terminology) seem to imply. I am willing to go along with his suggestion; but – as I interpret Prebisch's point in relation to my own – it is not the overall level of savings observed in the 'privileged consumption society' that is a matter of contention, but rather the fact that it is the socio-political context in which these events take place that leads savings to be redirected mainly towards financing the public sector deficit rather than new investment in machinery and equipment.

Nor is my tentative explanation contradicted by the fact that official data on employment in both manufacturing and the tertiary sectors of most LDCs are seriously underestimated, in that they fail to catch all the so-called informal activities that proliferate in the large metropolitan areas of those countries (underestimation being probably higher in the tertiary sectors due to the prevalence of personal services). The participants in all informal activities – whether classifiable as manufacturing or tertiary – are usually excluded from the potential gains that I have described above and constitute the true 'lumpen-proletariat' of the developing world. Some – very few indeed compared to their number – are occasionally drawn into the manufacturing sectors as unskilled labour: this is why we tend to find industrial wages moving at a relatively slower pace in most LDCs as compared to the rest of the industrialised world. Instead, mobility into the organised tertiary sector appears to be very limited, thus helping to preserve the privileges of those who are already in it. There indeed exists a very profound segmentation between the organised or semi-organised labour market and the informal labour market. And it is such a deep segmentation that to a large extent determines income determination and distribution in the tertiary sectors. My hypothesis is that labour market segmentation in many LDCs is merely a reflection of social stratification, as it is dictated by the needs for social equilibrium.

Let me now turn back to what I find the main theme of Professor Tsuru's contribution: in the early stages of Japan's industrialisation the political system did have a clear-cut strategy laid out: breaking the privileges of the feudal classes and at the same time making use of the traditional values to lead the way towards rapid development.

If my observations of these patterns of income distribution among countries of the less developed world are grounded, they seem to indicate that, to the extent that replacing or modifying the traditional social order is a necessary condition for development, the task of breaking it up and laying out new strategies of development is perhaps more difficult in today's world than it was in Japan in the course of the Meiji restoration.

Addresses to the Final Session

Economic Development in the Coming Years

H. Flores de la Peña

MEXICO

It is clear that the first task of economists in poor countries, if they are to study the possibility of achieving a high and sustained rate of future growth, is to analyse the essential problems of development in all their aspects, institutional, social and political, and thus break through the barriers imposed by traditional economics, so as to obtain better results in the future.

If we are to avoid falling into the errors of the past in trying to solve the problem of providing productive occupation for the labour force, we must start from historical experience. As things are, the limits to any increase of employment manifest themselves at a very low level of activity. Employment hardly begins to expand before it is checked by the foreign balance or by pressures from inflation.

Contemporary economic science is suffering from a serious loss of recognition as a consequence of its ineffectiveness and its failure to solve either the problems of unemployment or those of inflation. Since the days of Keynes every economist has known how to increase income without resorting to war. But no economist knows how to stop inflation, since an overall theory of income and production is conspicuously missing in economic thought.

We must at the same time be careful about adopting 'fashionable' economic approaches, such as those of the 'new economists'. Their ideas are not new. These are the same people who have not only made economics superficial but have also given it an ideological tone which dominates its scientific content. Instead of handling their scientific tools properly they take the easy way of ideological dogma and out-dated arguments.

In any analysis of the causes of poverty we have to move away from these simplistic formulations. The causes of poverty cannot be reduced to shortage of capital and lack of technical knowledge. We must never lose sight of the facts that:

(i) the basic objective of economic policy is to provide paid employment for everyone;
(ii) a steady growth of income and its better distribution is the foundation of democracy and freedom;
(iii) the political stability of democratic governments rests on the success of their policies in raising the standard of living of the majority that put them into power.

The study of the causes of poverty and of the policies that can overcome it is made more important and more urgent by the following factors:

(i) the frustration created by two decades of international rhetoric regarding the possibility of achieving more rapid growth;
(ii) the urgent need for economic, social and political reasons for finding a solution of the problems of underdevelopment;
(iii) the world economic situation, which is increasingly unfavourable to the development of poor countries.

Great hopes have been created during the past twenty years of the possibility of achieving a high and steady rate of growth, sustained by an expanding world trade, by technical and financial aid from the rich countries, and by a sound and orderly international financial system, operating in accordance with norms of good behaviour laid down by the international lending organisations.

Unfortunately, the realities have been very different from the expectations. And apart from that, the development policies advocated by the rich countries and the international agencies have been chosen for political reasons rather than for their intrinsic merits.

Since rich countries have possessed abundant capital and technical knowledge, poverty has been seen as a problem of scarce capital and lack of technical knowledge. Other more important factors have been ignored. This has given the international agencies a prestige and power of which they had never dreamed. It has made them arbiters in the distribution of an ever-increasing volume of financial and technological resources. More important, it has given them the opportunity to expand without limit an international bureaucracy which is coming to be regarded as an obstacle to development.

As failures have multiplied, they have been misinterpreted to prove that the type of government and the form of its institutions have been the key factors in the explanation of economic backwardness. If only the advantages of free enterprise could have been discovered and adopted in a country, more rational use of capital and technology would have been a consequence. Only a small government activity would have been needed for this. Thus 'a top-heavy and expensive bureaucracy could have been prevented from frustrating the entrepreneur that is concealed in all of us'.

The facts have shown, however, that in reality it is not the size of the government that creates poverty. People are poor because they are excessively exploited by an entrepreneurial class whose power to do this is not equalled in the most capitalist of the rich countries. Poverty persists because any additional income goes to the landowner or the owner of the business and there is no incentive for the individual to increase his productivity.

The alternatives are neither a strong state nor a weak state. They concern the forms of intervention of the state, bearing in mind it is necessarily strong and that dictatorship is no substitute for an efficient economy.

Once again the hard facts have insisted on falsifying these hopes. Problems of trade and a trade war arose in which we were on the losing side. Indebtedness made it impossible for a poor country to use the whole of its export earnings. The situation grew worse with the worldwide inflation of the 1970s. There was financial disaster created by those who buy everything on credit with a promissory note with no date of payment and no stability of value. And finally the rise of oil prices extinguished all hope of growth in the poverty-stricken countries.

The need to achieve significant results quickly is moreover a consequence of population growth on the one hand and of the spread of education and the mass media on the other.

Without more rapid economic growth, universal poverty is made permanent by population growth. If rarely and intermittently faster growth is achieved, it will quickly be overtaken by population growth. This has brought the underdeveloped countries into the familiar vicious circle of poverty as a major obstacle to change and improvement.

Success in breaking out of this will largely depend on a fuller awareness of higher standards of life and higher levels of education. It is the mass media as much as education that makes people dissatisfied with their existing standards, and determined to improve them. They emigrate to foreign countries or from the rural areas to the cities. They form there the vast slums of the big cities of the third world. Yet despite everything these urban marginals live better than in the rural areas they have left. But they form compact groups of dissatisfied people who may become on the one hand the means to greater progress, or on the other hand the cause of greater political instability and even the sufferers of severe repression, should development fail to take place.

In the past all religions have been based on acceptance of poverty. Today, the rich countries offer a very inadequate substitute in the worship of the institutions of the free market and of the absence of state intervention. The constant reiteration of these dogmas is the best means of concealing the reality of the exploitation of man by man.

In the last few months it has become increasingly clear that for some years ahead we shall be living under the shadow of unemployment, inflation, the contraction of world trade and international monetary disorder. This does not augur well for the development of poor countries during the coming decade.

The ability of the underdeveloped countries to cope with these problems is virtually non-existent. Their effect on the countries concerned is in inverse proportion to the level of development and the openness of the economy. A policy of austerity will only work as a weapon against inflation if, firstly, real wages fall when there is unemployment, so that all can work at a much lower wage, and if, secondly, profits are reduced through supply and demand – that is if prices cannot be manipulated by agreement between entrepreneurs. It is difficult enough for these conditions to be satisfied in a democratic regime where class-conscious trade unions exist and trade agreements may not be wholly prevented.

If the rich countries succeed with their new mercantilist policies, they will end by shifting part of the increased cost of oil imports on to the poor countries and thus reduce the total level of world economic activity. In economics what one gains another loses.

I believe that all strong countries ought to be interested in bringing some rationality into the world monetary system. At the same time regional measures can be of great value in isolating some markets from the disorders of others.

As to the energy problem, which has very seriously increased all the difficulties of poor countries, much might be done to help them with schemes similar to those introduced by Mexico and Venezuela for Central America and the Caribbean.

But until the rich countries abandon their rhetoric of good intentions and decide to take responsible steps to rationalise the use of oil, the world will continue to head towards disaster. If this decade is the decade of expensive oil, the decade of the 1990s, before alternative sources become available, will be the decade of oil scarcity. What price shall we then have to pay for oil?

Whatever the answer, the outcome will be determined not only by the competence of economists but also by the political will to carry through the policies that are framed. We cannot hope to have a modern economic structure combined with archaic social and political structures.

More generally it can be said that, if the rate of development is to be both high and steady, a proper balance must be kept between all the different sectors of the economy. For the level and continuity of growth will be determined by the slowest growing main sector of the economy. In a modern society all the privileges of a traditional society cannot be preserved. But capital, unfortunately, is more ready to lose everything than to make the smallest voluntary concession of its privileges.

As Nicholas Kaldor has rightly shown, the first essential for development is that there should be a desire for development in the community as a whole. This will exist only if workers, both in rural and in urban areas, have an incentive to share in the process of development. And this in turn will only come about if the additional income generated is increasingly shared with them.

The proposals of the poor countries for a new international economic order may appear unrealistic to economists of developed countries. This may be true. But I would like to point out two things in our defence. First, poverty and hunger do not create the best environment for dispassionate and careful analytical reasoning. Second, the economists of the rich countries have not provided better alternative solutions for a problem that affects us all, rich and poor alike.

Finally, it remains only for me to point out that if the group of rich countries is incapable of doing something to help the many who are poor, even less will they be able to secure their own national survival. For it is ingenuous to suppose that the rich can survive in a world that is impoverished. Political instability and perhaps terrorism are only the demonstrations of this social law.

The World Economic Outlook

Lord Kaldor
CAMBRIDGE, ENGLAND

I have been asked to sum up my views on the economic outlook of the world in twenty minutes from the point of view of an older economist who has lived through many cycles of intellectual fashion (and of general waves of optimism and pessimism) and thus, if only on account of age, has had more occasion to rethink the ways of approaching the economic problems of the world than those of you who have the enviable misfortune of being younger. The one clear result I have reached is that is no use applying established 'models' or methods of thought when confronted with a new situation that was largely unforeseen. You must start by asking which was the particular feature that your previous method failed to take on board. As Keynes once said, the difficult and the creative part in the progress of thought lies in discarding old ideas, far more difficult task than inventing new ones.

Professor Samuelson, in the remarkable paper which he presented the beginning of this conference, reminded us of Keynes' basic optimism when he thought, long before he produced *The General Theory Employment*, that the economic problem, the problem of want due material insufficiencies or scarcities could be solved, with luck, in a few generations. While some of his predictions, as Samuelson has shown proved remarkably successful in foretelling the rate of economic progress of the golden decades – the period between 1950 and 1970 – horizon did not really extend beyond that lucky corner of the world which comprised, apart from England, only the states of northwestern Europe and of North America. Though the post-war golden decades meant higher geometric growth rates for the poor and the rich countries alike, the differences between them became larger in absolute terms and widened more rapidly.

In terms of aspirations, the tensions resulting from greater awareness of this contrast – which was a by-product of the revolution in communications: intellectual, pictorial and physical – became very much greater, both between rich and poor countries and between rich and poor classes within countries.

There was a time, not so long ago, when it was widely believed that poverty was mainly the result of capital shortage – meaning by that, lack of plant and machinery per head – and that it was only necessary to teach the poor the virtues of saving (and of learning), and to teach the rich to help the poor by generous grants and long-term loans and technical assistance, in order to bring all mankind to the same standards of well-being within a measurable distance of time. (Maybe some people still believe in this – it follows automatically from the paradigm which regards capital and labour as *the* two factors of production.) In my view nothing could have been more naïve. The resource-endowment which was the real constraint, was not lack of capital, so-called (for plenitude of capital is the result more than the cause of successful development) but the limitations imposed by natural resources, whether those derived from the soil or from beneath the soil (or the sea). For the world population as a whole to attain Western European or North American living standards, the products annually extracted from nature in the form of basic foodstuffs, basic industrial materials or minerals or fossil fuels, would need to be increased many times—perhaps five- or sixfold. One need not be a close follower of Professor Meadows or of the Club of Rome to realise that this is an impossible goal.

I wonder whether many economists have thought seriously about the question of the universal prediction of all classical economists – from Adam Smith through Ricardo to John Stuart Mill – that, on account of the scarcity of land and natural resources, all economic growth must some time come to an end; and on the way to this end, an ever-rising proportion of labour will need to be devoted to satisfying the basic human need for food, leaving only a diminishing proportion for all other needs. The reality, since Ricardo, has been the very opposite. The proportion of labour absorbed in agriculture has become less and less, while the surplus of agricultural production over agricultural self-consumption – which Smith regarded as the indispensable prerequisite for employing labour in the production of industrial goods and services (including those required by the Sovereign) – has become enormously larger, and this has happened in spite of the fact that industrial development, wherever it has occurred, has been attended by a huge population explosion.

138   *Human Resources and Developmen*

Ricardo, it is true, left himself a loophole; the great Law o Diminishing Returns, which ultimately rules over everything, can b suspended for a time by what he called 'improvements in the arts o cultivation'. In retrospect this was the greatest understatement in th whole classical literature. The improvements in these arts – in othe words, land-saving or natural resource-saving inventions an innovations – not only suspended the operation of this great Law, bu made it appear as if it had never existed. It banished it from the scen altogether. And this happened despite the fact that the other main for of technical progress, namely labour-saving inventions, also mad enormous strides through the discovery of new machines and new way of utilising non-human power, which in turn meant that a given supp of industrial inputs, whether the products of agriculture or of minin required so much less labour for their conversion into finished goods. despite all this, the last two hundred years have witnessed such a enormous increase in non-agricultural employment, both absolute and proportionately to the whole, this must mean that, contrary popular belief, the natural-resource-saving aspect of the progress human knowledge was quantitatively superior to the labour-savi aspect. Without that superiority, labour-saving inventions by themse ves (whether they implied the substitution of machinery for labour or t better exploitation of economies of scale with the growth of market would have meant a total demand for labour in the secondary a tertiary sectors. For output could not have grown faster than t increase in man's powers over nature permitted; if the saving of labour the conversion or processing of raw products had progressed at an ev faster rate, non-agricultural employment opportunities would ha fallen and not risen.

Of course, excepting the lucky countries during their good perio there has never been full employment, in the sense of there being frustrated applicants for jobs: no excess supply in the labour market. the vast amount of disguised unemployment in both agriculture a services is also taken into account (and this existed in even the wealthi countries in their most successful periods), one is forced to conclude t the land-saving bias in technical progress, however important, was n great enough. It could not increase the supply of primary products f enough to keep pace with the growth of population as well as with progress in labour-saving technology. And even before the histo break of 1973, unemployment became steadily more prominent in mo if not all, of the poorer countries of the world – the new jobs crea failed to keep pace with the rising numbers in need of work. And latest phase of technical progress, which some regard as a technical revolution, that of the computer and the microprocessor, is of course far more labour-saving than land-saving in character.

The worldwide problem of unemployment, which was getting steadily worse long before the events of 1973 and after, according to the reports of the World Bank, was greatly aggravated by the remedies adopted to fight inflation, by what I would like to call the curse of monetarism. This is an intellectual disease which has spread like wildfire in the last five to ten years, like some crazy Californian cult. It is based on an extremely crude and faulty diagnosis but with a strong appeal to the self-interested and to the semi-educated, the success of which is likely to aggravate greatly the social tensions and instabilities resulting from increasing inequalities and increasing unemployment.

I have no time on this occasion to analyse why the world became increasingly polarised between rich and poor countries as a result of the very success of capitalism. It must suffice to say that one important cause of this division is the differences in the way markets operate as between primary producers on the one hand and manufacturers and the service industries on the other. Competition in primary production has normally meant that the benefits of cost reductions due to technical progress have been passed on to the buyer in the form of lower prices, whereas in the case of manufacturing industry the benefits of increases of productivity have, on the whole, been retained by the producers in the form of both higher wages and higher profits. This is a feature which has been largely ignored by economists, with notable exceptions such as Raul Prebisch or Arthur Lewis. The obvious remedy to this state of affairs for primary producers is to form a cartel and raise the price to what the traffic can bear. But for various reasons, until OPEC came along, no such successful cartel could be established on a durable basis.

Since the world demand for oil is price-inelastic, the optimal monopoly price is vastly different from the cost price. But as the prices of industrial goods are cost-determined, irrespective of the relation of supply and demand, the effect of raising oil prices by 400 per cent within a few months was to generate a rise in industrial prices which in turn led both to faster increases in wages and to further bouts of price increases by OPEC members.

The response of the developed countries to these events in recent years was to contract their economies by fiscal and monetary measures, leaving the non-oil-producing developing countries in the unfortunate position of providing the counterpart, in the form of deficits, to the financial surpluses of the OPEC countries. These huge deficits have so

far been financed by the big private banks of the developed countries o
Europe and the United States (the sums involved are far too large fo
official institutions like the IMF to cope with) but on an increasingl
precarious basis.

The situation may lead in a matter of a few years to an internationa
banking collapse unless that collapse is averted (as it very probabl
would be) by large-scale interventions of the major central banks of th
world to rescue their main customers. Such a development, though n
doubt regarded with horror by the financially orthodox, would be
mixed curse. For it would also signal the end of monetarism.

Nonetheless, the dangers to the world economy resulting from thes
trends are quite unpredictable. The more one thinks of the situation th
more one feels that the outcome could be disastrous. Yet somethin
quite unforeseen could always occur that would falsify such di
predictions. On past form economists were more often wrong when the
prophesised disaster than when they saw the future in rosy colours.
might happen for example that some unexpected new invention wi
make natural resources, particularly energy-providing resources, fa
more plentiful and that this will make both developed and developir
countries bold enough to expand their economies, so as to exploit th
new opportunities.

But we must not forget that all the time there lurks the threat o
annihilation through a major nuclear war. There is no logical reaso
why this should occur or should be expected to occur, except for the fa
that we are in the middle of an armaments race and in the past suc
armaments races have invariably ended in wars, sooner or later. There
also the basic trait of *homo sapiens* (a trait which I am told it shares wi
rats but no other species) of always wanting to engage in combat wi
others of its own kind and not, as is the case with other mammals, wi
species of a different kind. Man's inborn passion to kill has not be
sensibly abated by all the achievements of civilisation, religion
education: witness the extraordinary increase of terrorist murders whi
afflicts rich and poor countries alike. The difference is that up to no
man did not possess the technical know-how for total self-destructio
Nuclear power has changed all that, and it cannot be excluded that a
result *homo sapiens* will become extinct, just as the dinosaurs did
earlier phases of the evolution of life. His disappearance would caus
great set back to the evolution of life in this planet, but sooner or late
new species will arise which, in accordance with the Darwinian laws
natural selection, will be free of the desire for self-destruction, whi
alone could cause his disappearance.

Addresses to the Closing Session, in the Presence of his Excellency José López Portillo, President of Mexico

Address to Final Session[1]

Victor L. Urquidi

(PRESIDENT-ELECT OF THE INTERNATIONAL
ECONOMIC ASSOCIATION)

The Sixth World Congress of Economists held under the auspices of the
International Economic Association and the National College of
Economists of Mexico today comes to a close. It is a great honour for me
to have been elected by the Council to be President of the association for
the next three years, of an organisation that counts among its members
fifty-four national societies or associations from all the continents and
which brings together economists of many different schools of thought.
In taking office today, I wish first to pledge myself to endeavour without
fail, with the help of the distinguished Vice-President, Professor Franco
Modigliani, and the other members of the Executive Committee, to
enlarge and intensify the implementation of our organisation's objectives. During the last three years, this task has been shouldered by
the eminent and greatly respected economist, Dr Shigeto Tsuru, and
it is particularly pleasant to record the gratitude of all members
of our association for his wise and efficient furtherance of our activities.

As a reflection of the growing interest of many members of the
association, both old and new, in participating in the international
debates on economic science by contributing new ideas and new
experiences, an economist from a developing country has for the first
time been elected President of the association. I am therefore also
conscious of the responsibility which I am assuming to help ensure that
the debate shall be both at a high level and scientifically rigorous, and
that it shall relate also to the problems and realities for mankind that we

[1] Translated from the Spanish.

are all perceiving with increasing intensity. For this I rely on the support of the member societies and associations and on further active participation on their part, and I hope myself to develop closer contacts with the scientific communities of the different regions. Those who know me will be aware that one of my traits is a sense of balance, and at the same time, a certain dynamic spirit, and that I consequently view with optimism the possibilities offered by our association of generating greater international understanding and support for our science, not only for the sake of the science as such but also for the sake of its application.

To my Mexican colleagues, and to the Mexican National College of Economists in particular, I wish to express my appreciation for their support and the hope that I may contribute to their further participation in the activities of the International Economic Association.

Established thirty years ago, under the auspices of UNESCO, our association has as its main purpose 'to initiate and co-ordinate measures of international collaboration designed to assist the advancement of economic knowledge'. To this end, conferences and seminars have been held in different parts of the world on a wide variety of subjects, both of theoretical interest and relating to the critique of theory, and to the application of theory; to different aspects of national, regional and international economic policy; to problems of market economies, mixed economies and economies organised under central planning processes; to a variety of general and specialised aspects of economics; to relations between economics and other disciplines or with problems of the social sciences, or between economics and the *problématique* deriving from the interplay of technological and cultural factors with socio-economic factors. I have been fortunate in taking part in a number of these meetings and I can testify to their high academic and professional level, the wide range of viewpoints presented and discussed, and the strong interest of the scientific community in the outcome of such meetings. The concrete evidence can be found, in any event, in the long list of publications of our association, edited with efficiency, enthusiasm and good sense by Professor Sir Austin Robinson, to whom we pay a well deserved and affectionate tribute for his hard editorial work over more than twenty-five years.

The association has also convened international congresses of economists with the purpose of enlarging the opportunities to present papers for discussion by a much wider number of economists than is possible in small specialised conferences. Usually, a central theme has been adopted that would be of interest both to the theoretical economists and to those concerned with real world problems as well as those with responsibilities for the planning or implementation of national or international policies. After the Fifth Congress in Tokyo in 1977, on 'Resources and Growth', it was logical to go on to consider the human element in development. Hence this Sixth Congress on 'Human Resources, Employment and Development'; for the human factor, as has been underlined by Professor Józef Pajestka at this meeting, is at the centre of our concern.

Economic activity, growth and development, broadly conceived, have it as their purpose to improve the lot of mankind, for man (and woman) is the actor and the beneficiary in such activity. Of course we know that it is not by economics alone that man lives, but the different schools of thought recognise the essential contribution to human well-being that is generated by the production of goods and services, their suitable distribution and the allocation of relatively scarce resources. To achieve these results, human beings, men and women, mainly those between the ages of 15 and 65, have historically organised themselves to create societies capable of promoting their welfare by the use of natural resources, their own labour and technology.

As is clear at this moment in the history of mankind, some societies have achieved this end better than others, and unfortunately in the last two hundred years, and especially in the last thirty, the differences or gaps have widened: almost two-thirds of the world's population suffer from a low standard of living, however that may be defined, and are unable to meet their basic needs, while the other third has attained levels which are not only adequate, but from many viewpoints irrational and even dangerous to the ecological balance of our planet. Yet within the developed nations broad sectors are lacking in material comforts and in living standards; while in the developing nations, with few exceptions, in spite of the efforts of many governments and of the wealth of available human and natural resources, the vast majority of people live as paupers, lacking adequate nutrition, education, housing and health, in a condition of acute inequality as compared with the middle and privileged classes.

At this time, if it were necessary to stress it, there are some 19 to 20 million people in the highly developed countries who are unemployed, and another 40 million in a condition of disguised unemployment, though beneficiaries of social security and health insurance. And in the developing nations, the overall number of openly unemployed, and of those in a state of disguised unemployment, underemployment or 'self-underemployment' is probably of the order of over 300 million, in almost all cases without benefit of social security. Thus some 25 to 30 per cent of the World's labour force is out of work or lacks really productive employment and a secure and acceptable minimum income.

To provide employment to that part of the population in the working-age groups who wish to work depends upon many factors: not only on the classical supply of and demand for labour, short-term or long-term, but also on a large variety of institutional, cultural and political and social organisation factors. It depends also, essentially, on the existence of a development strategy and the existence of favourable international conditions and relations. It must rely also, perhaps to an extent that is increasingly appreciated, on the generation, under whatever type of society, of suitable human motivations towards development, within a general and specific framework of ends and means. And it requires, above all, a process of societal understanding of the problems, possibilities and processes of advancement.

Our Sixth Congress has attempted to tackle many of these topics. It would be difficult to comment in brief terms on the richness of our debates, arising from over eighty invited papers and an even larger number of contributed papers submitted to the various sections of our congress. Consequently I shall limit myself to a few short ideas on the main topics, and subject to the proceedings that will later be published.

Participants have been concerned with basic concepts and their measurement: what do we understand by human resources, labour force, employment, underemployment, unemployment, in different contexts? How are they measured and monitored? It had to be admitted that imprecision prevails as to these matters; it was stressed that the human element, rather than being a 'resource' is the object and subject of mankind's activity; different forms of utilisation and application of labour have been considered, with different roles assigned to the state. As is frequent when dealing with theoretical and conceptual topics, no agreement has been reached, but without doubt new lines of thought have been opened. These discussions are by no means sterile.

The employment and unemployment situation in the developed countries was discussed in the Congress on the basis of authoritative papers, in order to clarify and define it. The developed nations, with very slow population growth and unfavourable cyclical trends, with subdivided labour markets, and faced with rapid technological change, are in the paradoxical situation of having a great productive potential but of not being able to generate the necessary employment. The short-run outlook, complicated by inflationary trends, does not seem to offer satisfactory and equitable solutions.

In the developing nations, structural causes of unemployment and underemployment are prevalent, with serious consequences for income distribution. In most cases, the development strategies are inadequate and structural change is absent or insufficient. To this must be added the externally originated factors which prevent or slow down the creation of employment to absorb the high rates of increase in the labour force. In many cases, the prospect is further aggravated by intense population change, both in terms of the overall average rates of increase and the extent of rural–urban migration. Thus it is increasingly difficult to achieve a balance in the various labour markets without giving rise either to underemployment or to very low wages, underprivileged or deprived employment sectors, and in general to social conditions that are morally and politically unacceptable. Technology, as is well known, is developed predominantly in the industrialised countries for the purpose, chiefly, of saving labour; in its transfer to the developing countries, such technology often provides only a small increase of employment. The developing countries have seldom been able to develop appropriate technological policies, and even encourage highly capital-intensive production processes through their fiscal, tariff and other policies.

These topics have been examined with special reference to Latin-American conditions in one of the sections of the Congress, with the participation not only of Latin-American economists but of those of other parts of the world. In addition, there has been discussion of employment structures, income distribution and employment policies in the various countries in the region, and among them Mexico, a country that has announced an overall development plan, a national employment plan and an industrial development plan, each containing specific employment targets.

As regards matters of international scope, attention has been paid to the characteristics, causes and consequences of migration, to trade policy, and especially to the negative impact on employment arising from the protectionist policies of the industrialised countries. Discussion has also taken place of the relation of short-term monetary policy to employment, it being noted that there is a need to affect not only demand but supply, as represented by infrastructure and productive capacity for the production of goods and services.

Finally, as is usual among economists concerned with the future, there has been discussion of papers on population and labour force projections, on manpower planning, on the role of education and training, on the impact of technology and on the participation of women in the labour force.

This has not been just another congress of the International Economic Association. It has been, so far as I could tell from three crowded days of intense discussion, a congress that will have marked the signs of a transition of economic science in the understanding of the real world in which we live, and towards new approaches and a new stage in the application of knowledge to the economic problems of our societies, both developed and underdeveloped, both market-economies and socialist economies. If this has been achieved, or is in the process of being achieved, the International Economic Association will have contributed to the hopes placed in the Congress by the international scientific community and, for obvious reasons, by the host country to which I belong.

Thank you, President José López Portillo, for your presence at this closing session and for your disinterested support to the development of economic science.

Thank you also, my fellow participants, for your valuable contribution to the activities of our association. To those of you who come from other countries, may I wish you a happy return home, and express the hope that we may see you again at the Seventh World Congress in 1983.

Address to Final Session

Manuel Aguilera Gómez

(PRESIDENT OF THE COLEGIO NATIONAL DE ECONOMISTAS MEXICO)

Today we complete our labours. The Local Organising Committee wishes to thank the Government of the Republic for the help that it has provided for the realisation of this event.

The addresses and discussions on the theme of the congress, 'Human Resources, Employment and Development', have taken place in an atmosphere of freedom and at a high academic level; the exchange of ideas and experiences between highly qualified economists has been animated by a search for the truth.

A deep concern regarding the present critical economic situation of the world economy has prevailed throughout the debates. The immediate post-war period had been a time of unparalleled economic expansion, both in terms of its intensity and dynamism and in terms of its duration. For a quarter of a century the industrialised centres had been rebuilding their economies and had entered into an epoch of consumption expansion to such levels and extremes that a revulsion from consumption had arisen in some of them.

For the majority of the human race, however, for the millions who inhabit the underdeveloped areas of our planet, access to the benefits of this immense technological progress was extremely limited and in some cases unknown to many of them.

We have to acknowledge that the increased welfare standards achieved in the industrial societies were not exclusively due to technological improvements but also to the massive transfer of economic surplus that undoubtedly contributed to their living standards. We must also acknowledge that behind this international division of labour lies an imposition on the developing areas of policy patterns based clearly on

149

hegemony. Indeed, the capital flows required to compensate the chronic deficits generated by such a growth pattern have been conditional on their adoption of an economic policy which, under the cover of supposed theoretical rationality, has in fact involved measures conducive to the perpetuation of dependency and inferiority. Thus, theoretical views designed to give scientific validity to economic policy norms which are morally and socially unacceptable, have been propagated only too often. In our own days, for example, certain academics, with the help of substantial financial backing, are engaged in a campaign to discredit the ability of states to allocate public expenditure, with the purpose of vindicating the freedom of the market as the ideal mechanism to optimise the use of resources. Those who propagate this thesis like to ignore the fact that, as is shown by experience, unrestricted freedom of the market leads to the suppression of all other freedoms. This thesis, as Professor Samuelson has recognised in our discussions here, inexorably leads to fascism.

Any attempt to forecast the future must start from a scientific understanding and a political recognition of the origins and nature of the present crisis. The bases and premises on which the economic growth of the immediate post-war period was grounded are now exhausted. On the one hand, North American hegemony has been challenged by the productive and commercial expansion of other industrialised areas; on the other, the expansion of the world economy has found a barrier in the underdeveloped countries. The crisis forces humanity to examine itself, just as it forces the world's intelligentsia and the world's political leaders to examine it. We are witnessing a battle for the widening of the economic frontiers of the industrialised areas in which the underdeveloped countries are passive victims, paying day-to-day tribute to the crisis.

It cannot be morally acceptable that accumulation at a world level should continue to feed on the fall in value of raw materials, on a transfer of financial resources that is dependent on existing geopolitical presuppositions, on the increase of the flood of available labour, on the present concentration of the benefits derived from technical progress, and on the uncontrolled private trans-nationalisation of economic policy decisions. It cannot be right that the weight of the adjustments in the international economy should take the form of the unrestricted opening of markets in the countries of intermediate development and the renunciation of their right to improve their terms of trade.

A claim has emerged in the Third World for the re-ordering of the world economy, and this has been taken up by the progressive sectors in industrial societies. It is the claim of millions of human beings who live in secular poverty, without a house, without a job, without any personal property. Respect for their condition as human beings will not become a reality, notwithstanding universal charters proclaiming morally valid rights, so long as the material basis of the relation of production and distribution on a world scale remains as it is today.

Members of the Congress, humanity demands peace: not simply as an absence of war, but as the expression of a political will to international co-operation. Mexico, like other countries, has joined in the United Nations forum to renew the universal dialogue conducing to the establishment of a new and more equitable system of international economic relations, starting with the rational management of energy resources.

We are conscious that the search for formulae for the reordering of the world economy is the responsibility of the political leaders of all countries. As professional economists and as members of the intelligentsia, we have, however, a moral obligation to use our personal influence to create an atmosphere able to affect favourably the political intentions of governments. If the ideas presented in the five days of discussions in this Congress have helped towards this aim, the material and human resources used in its organisation will have been amply justified. Thank you.

Index

Entries in the index in bold type under the names of participants in the conference indicate their Papers or Discussions of their Papers. Entries in italic type indicate contributions by participants to the Discussions.

DATE DUE

DEMCO 38-297